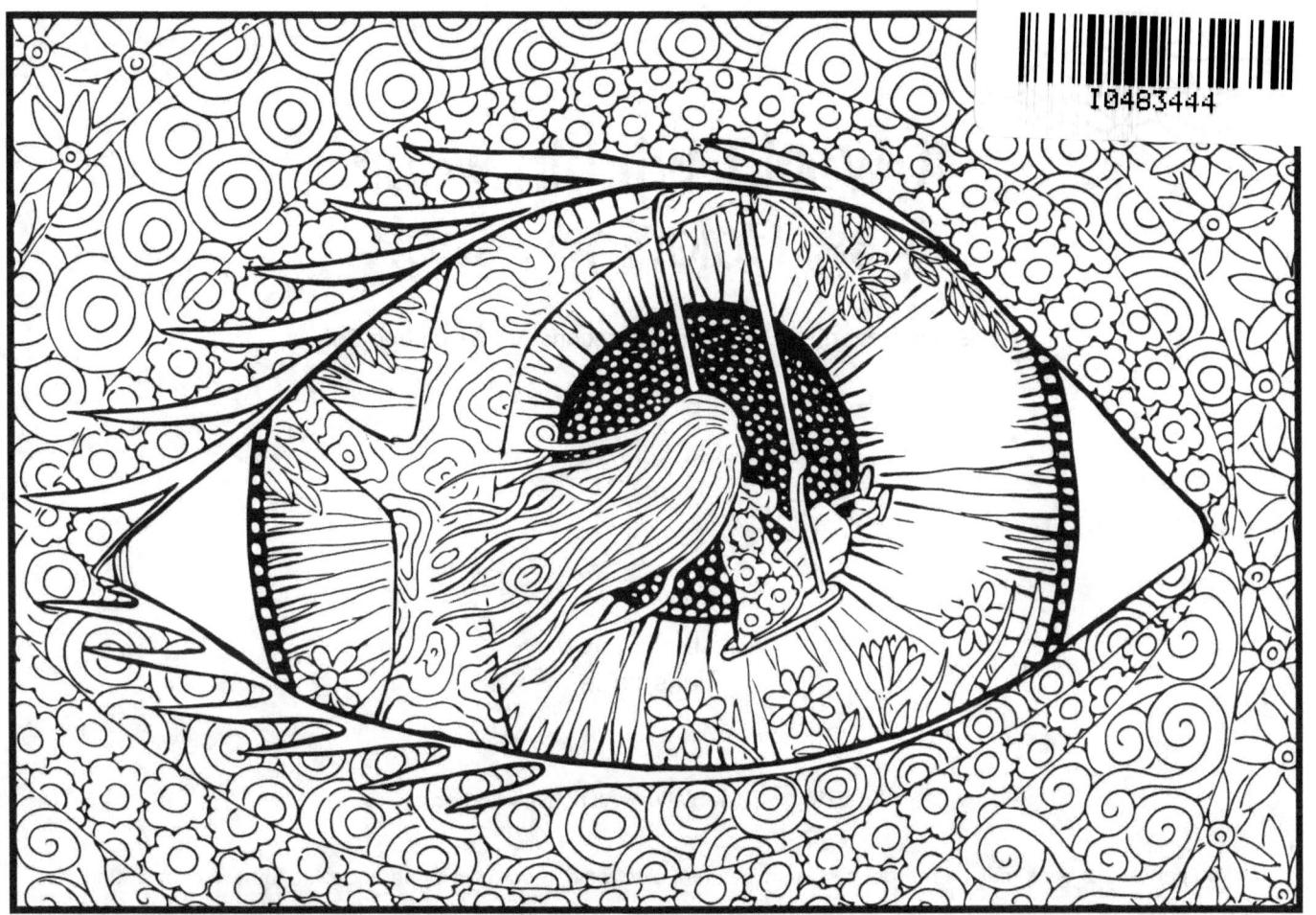

A World Within Your Eyes Coloring Book

Creative Patterned Eyes and Reflections Adult Coloring Book

'TRICK SLATTERY

COLOR ARTIST:

_____

A World Within Your Eyes Coloring Book

Creative Patterned Eyes and Reflections Adult Coloring Book

Published in 2016 by
Tricksplace

ISBN: 978-0-9938669-3-7

Created by 'Trick Slattery
www.TricksPlace.com

* This coloring book is dedicated to my loving wife Andie, who supported me throughout the creation process and whose vision influenced a number of these "eyes".

There is a "World Within Your Eyes" here: it's just waiting for you to add color and life!

Each of the patterned coloring pages represents a memory, feeling, idea or story, expressed as a reflection within a single eye. Eyes are considered to be windows to our innermost selves. They let in rays of light that create the shapes and colors we see all around us, they convey emotions and thoughts, and at the same time, they sometimes reflect amazing visions!

Express your intuition and creative energy in these visions! The eyes and patterns in this coloring book range from more whimsical simple to more complex with smaller nooks to fill, but you don't always need to stay within the lines!

The first few pages show a thumbnail sized image of the 32 unique eye illustrations - a visual table of contents! Following that are the full page, single-sided versions: rotate the book to view these landscape.

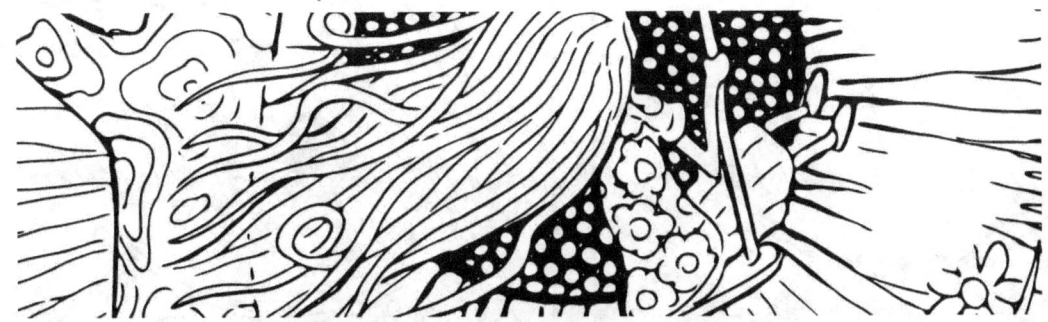

As a bonus, after the 32 full coloring pages, each of the images have been reduced to half page sizes, two eye images to a single-sided page. These allow you to color the same image in a different way or easily cut them out and take them with you to color separately (use a fine tip as the nooks will be smaller).

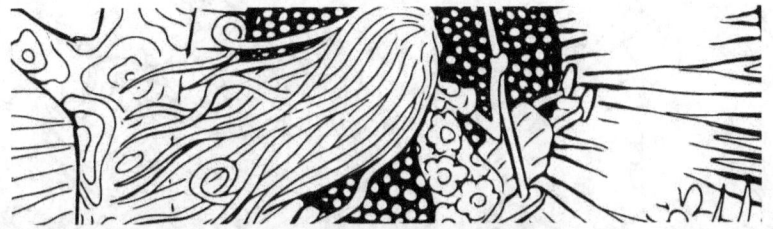

Though the illustrations are single-sided, protect the pages under the one you are working on by sliding a blank sheet of paper between the page you are coloring and the next image underneath it. This will protect other pages from hard colored pencil indents, etc. If you use markers or gel pens you may want to use more than one inserted page, or even cardstock, as wet media may seep through.

The images have a large margin so you can easily color the full image without being too near the spine of the book. This also gives you room to cut out the page and frame it! If you are using an X-acto knife, make sure to protect the pages underneath with cardboard or cardstock that you will not cut through.

 SHARE YOUR COLORED WORK! After you have colored in a page, if you want to - scan it in and share it on social media with the hashtag of #tricksplace and #eyecoloring. Please do not post or share uncolored pages. Also, join this dedicated facebook group and share there: facebook.com/groups/TricksPlaceColoring/

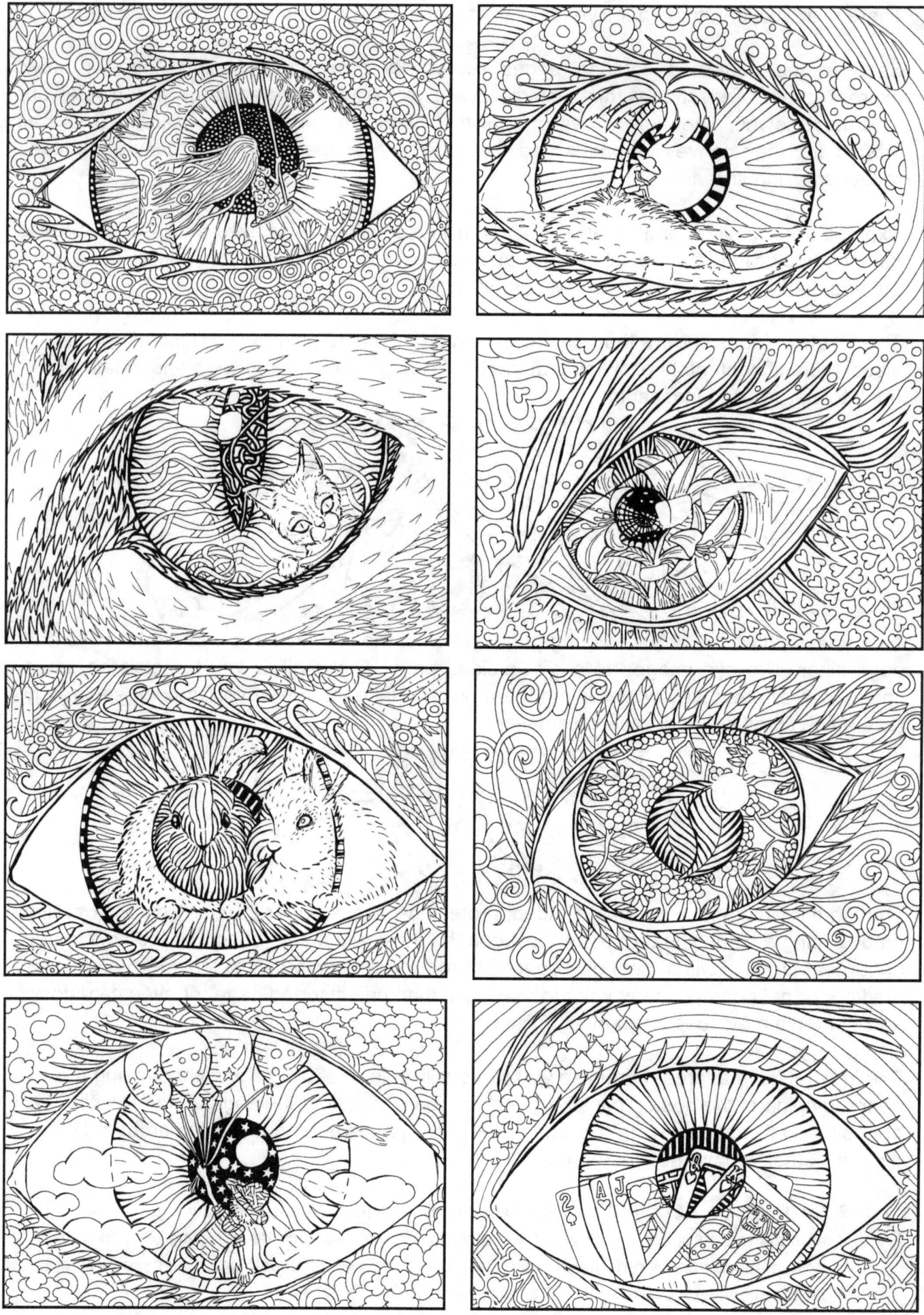

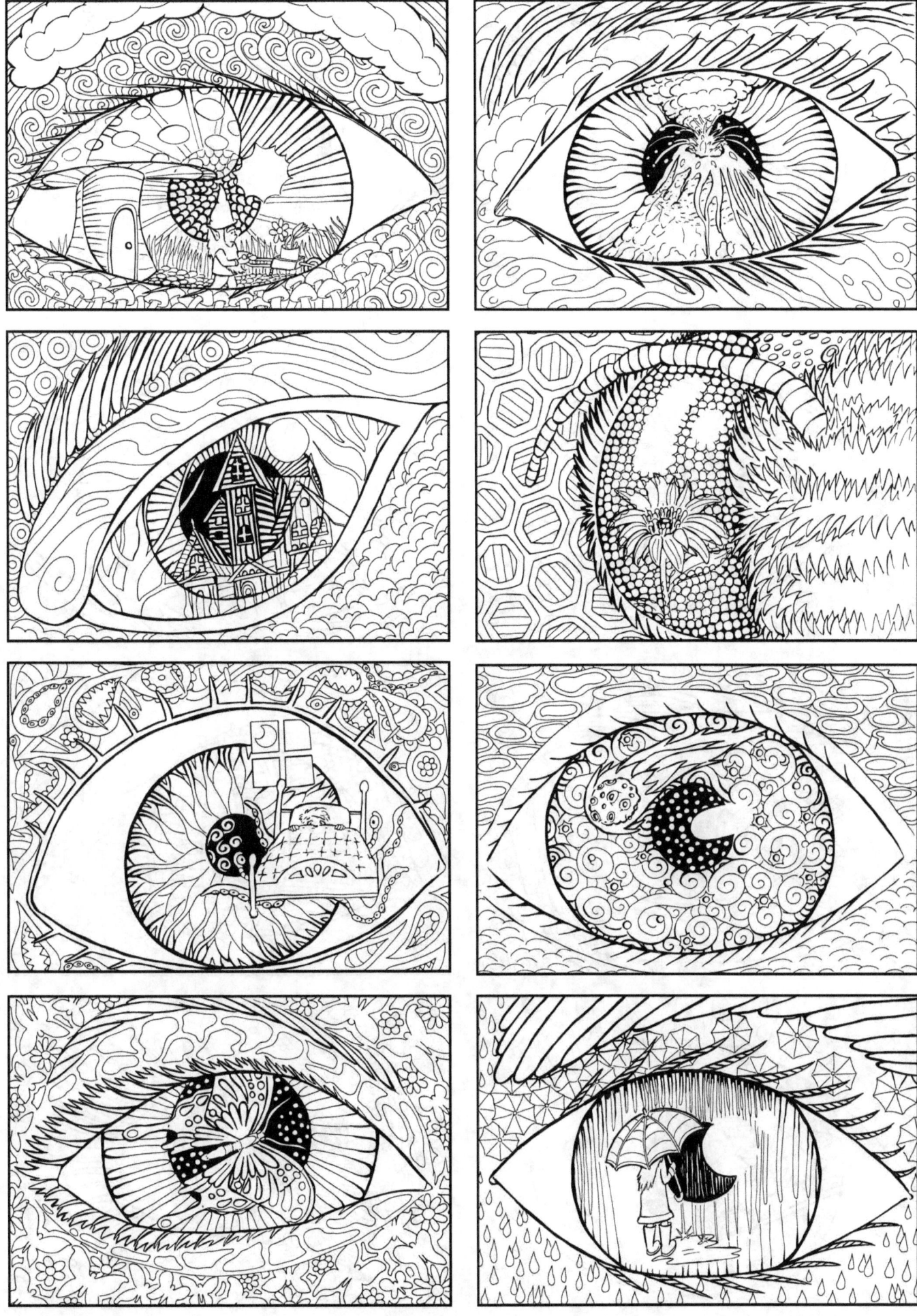

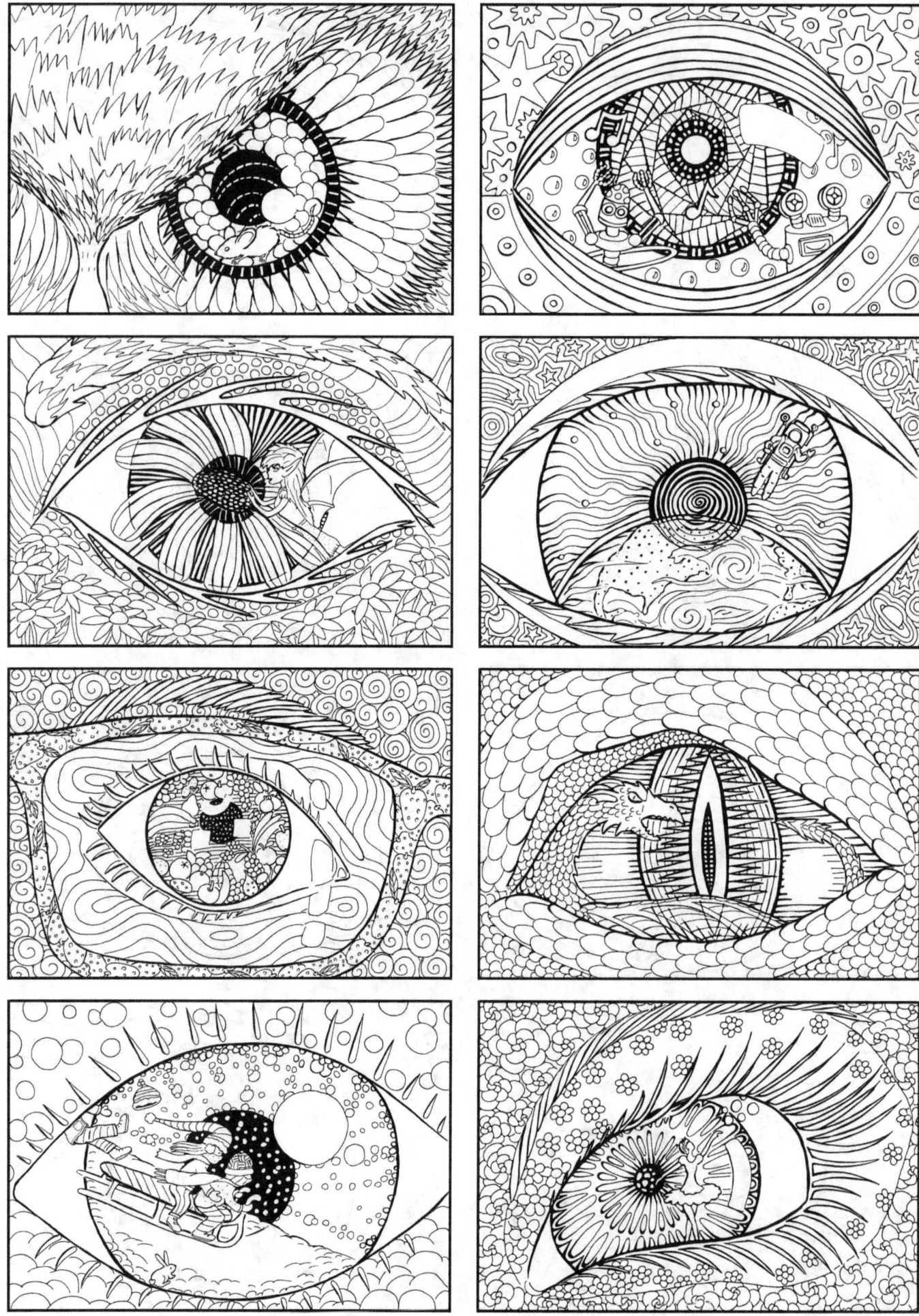

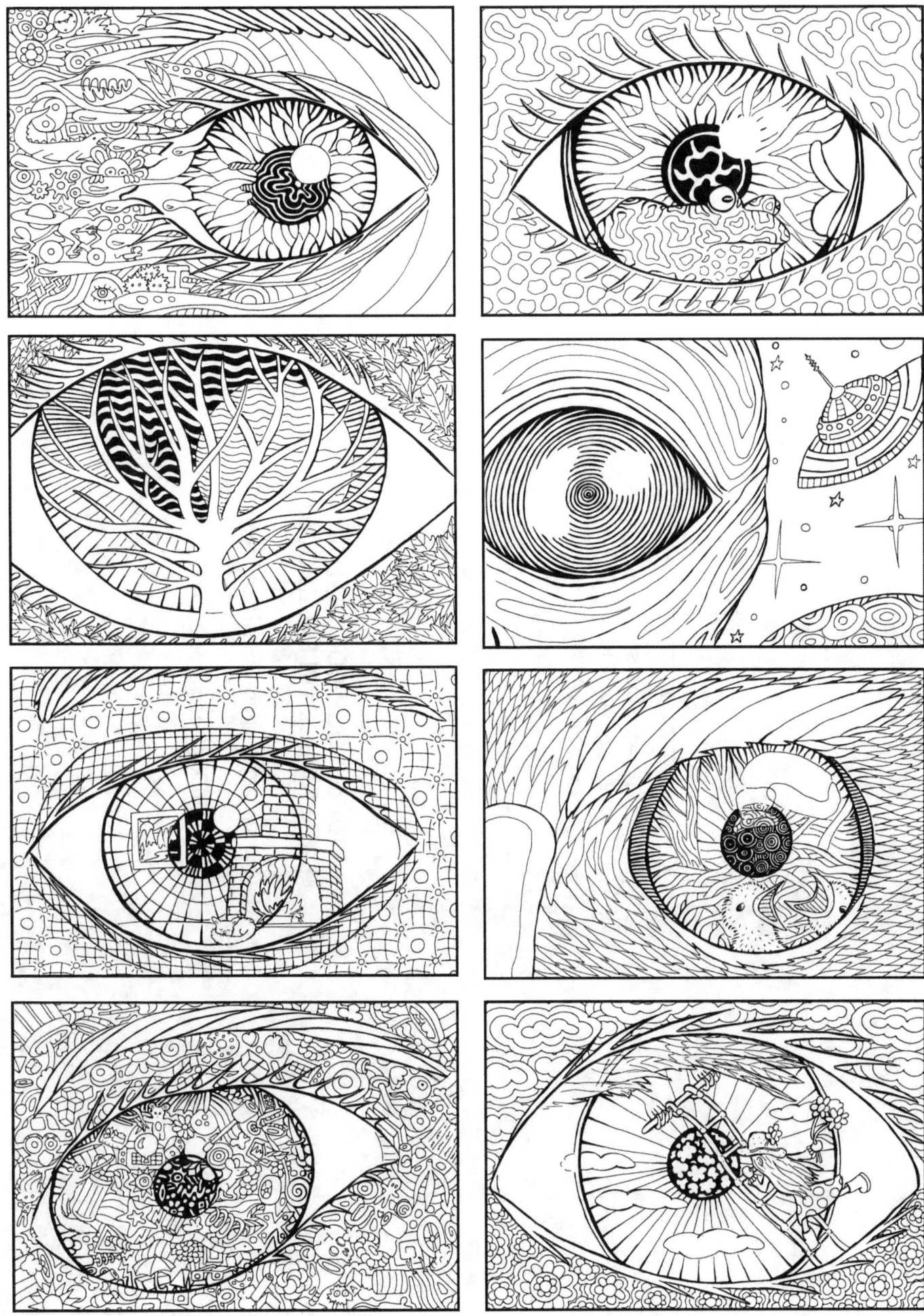

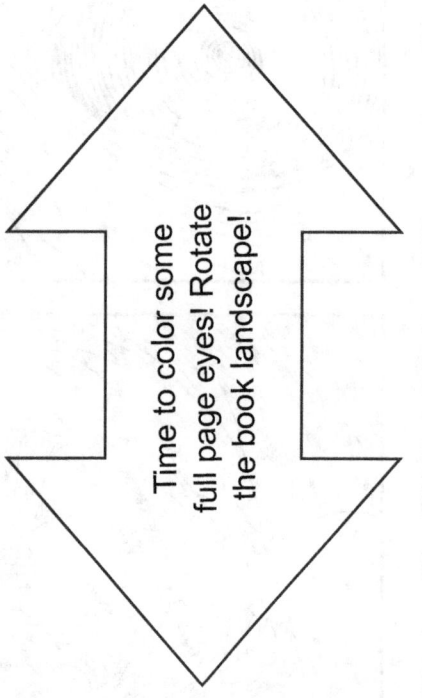

Time to color some full page eyes! Rotate the book landscape!

SHARE YOUR COLORED IN
MASTERPIECE ON FACEBOOK!

Facebook.com/groups/TricksPlaceColoring/

#tricksplace #eyecoloring

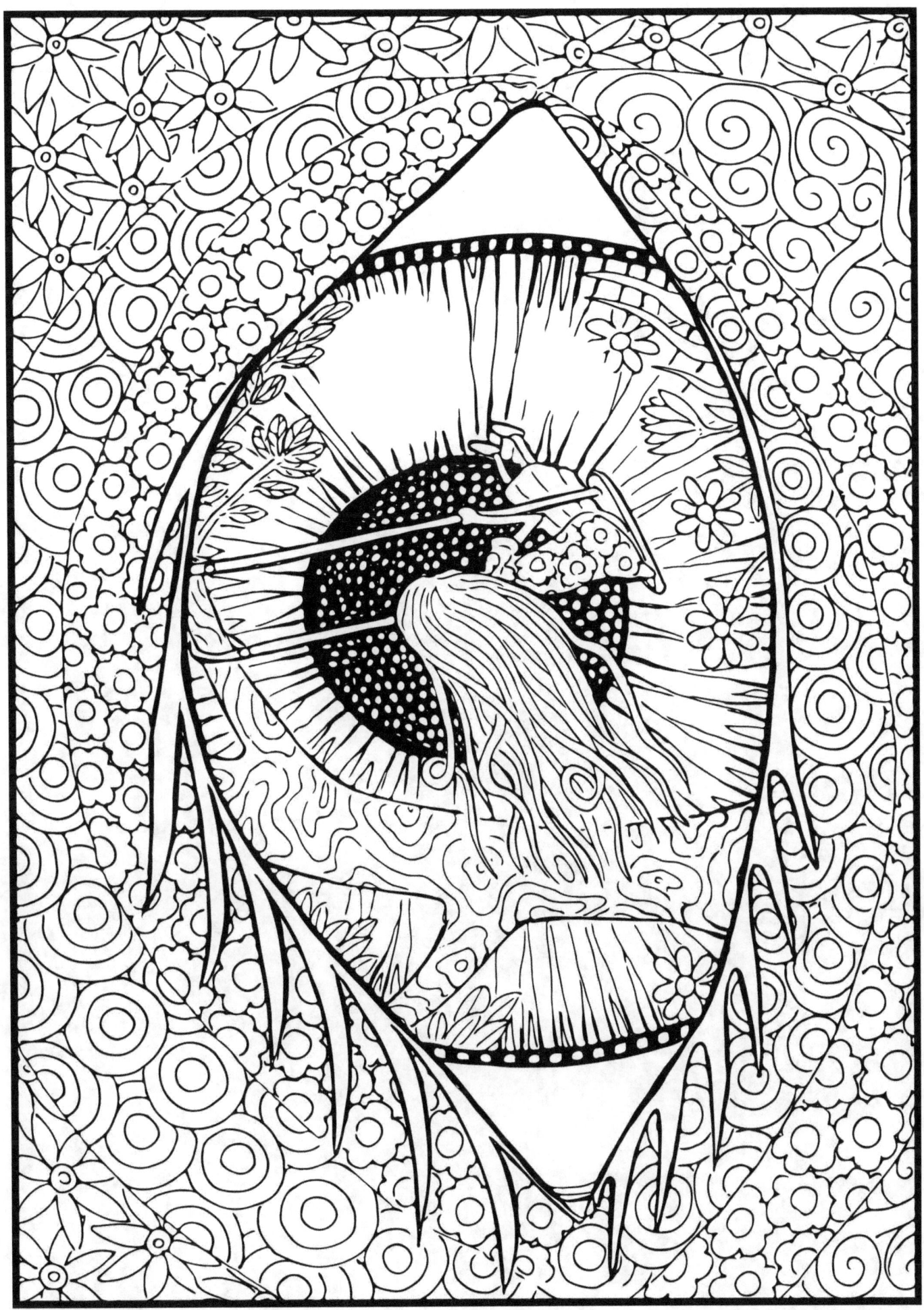

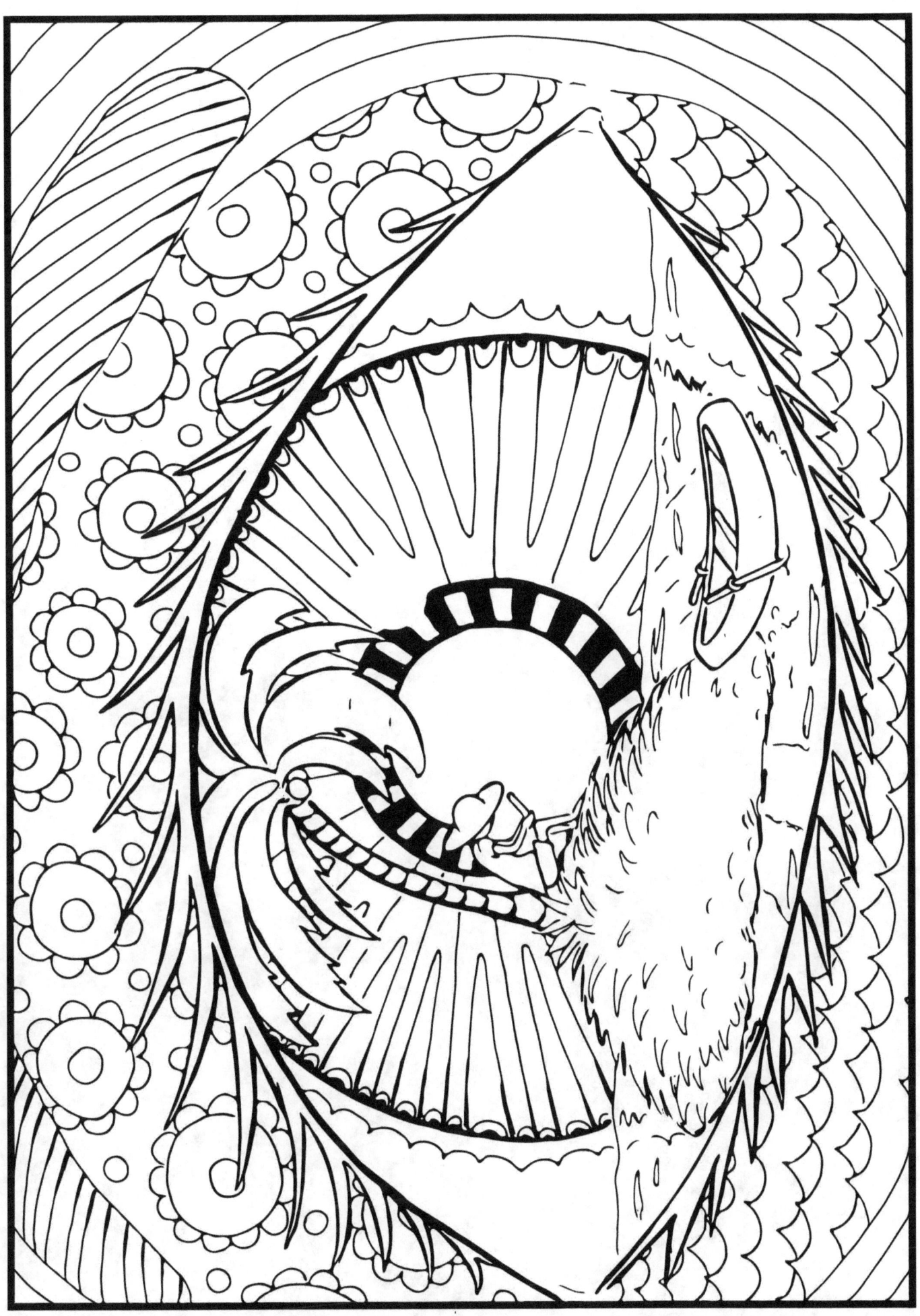

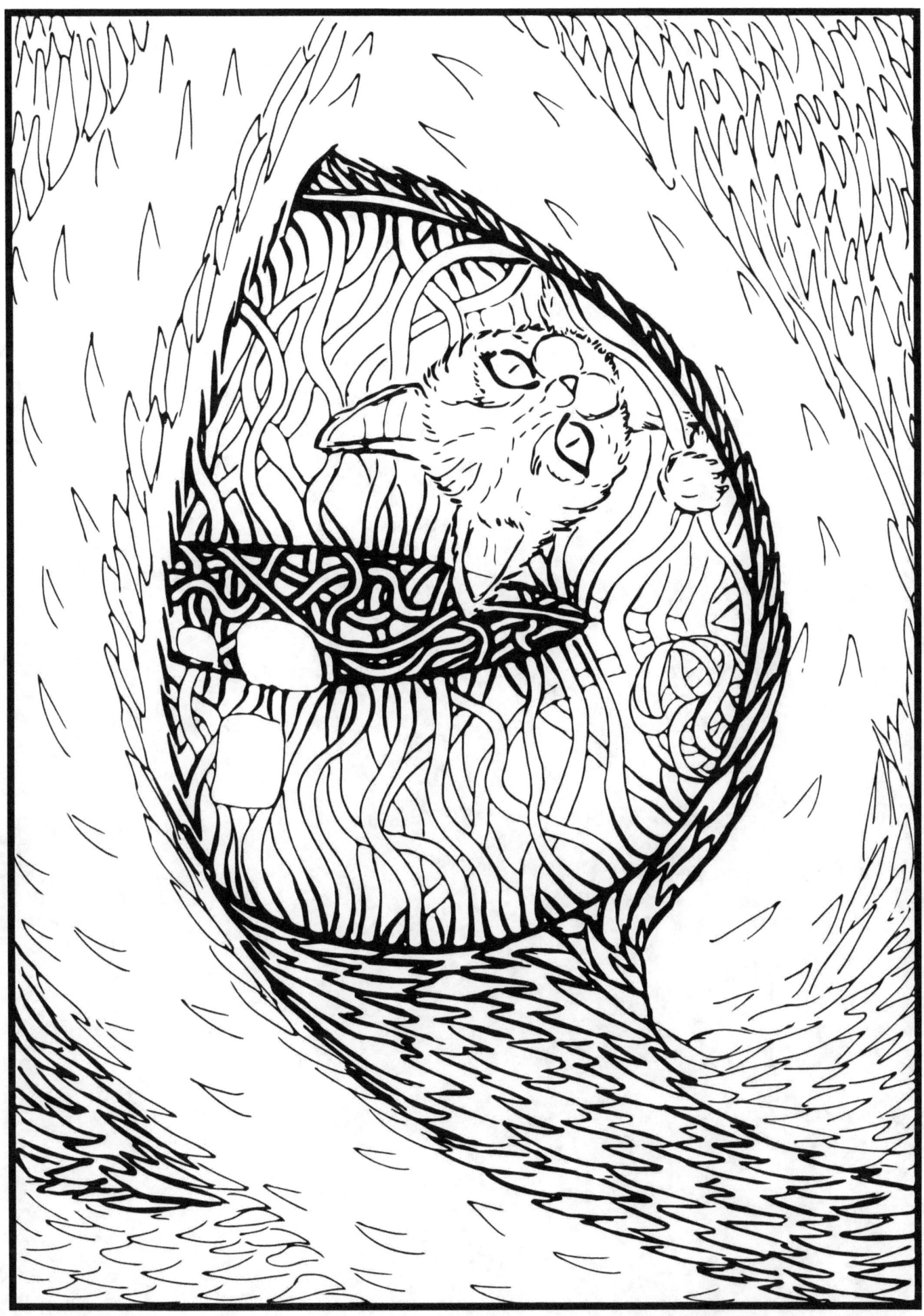

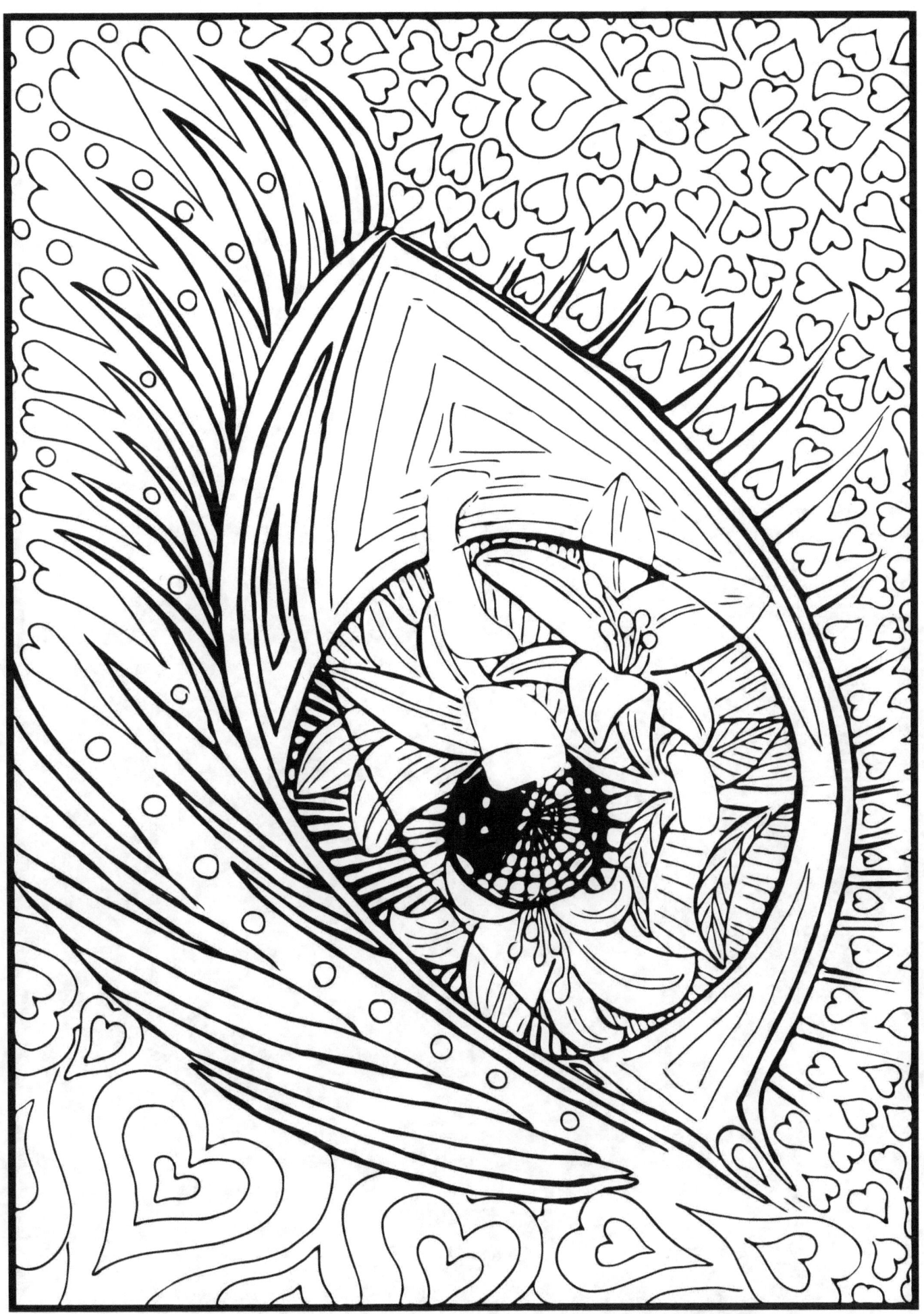

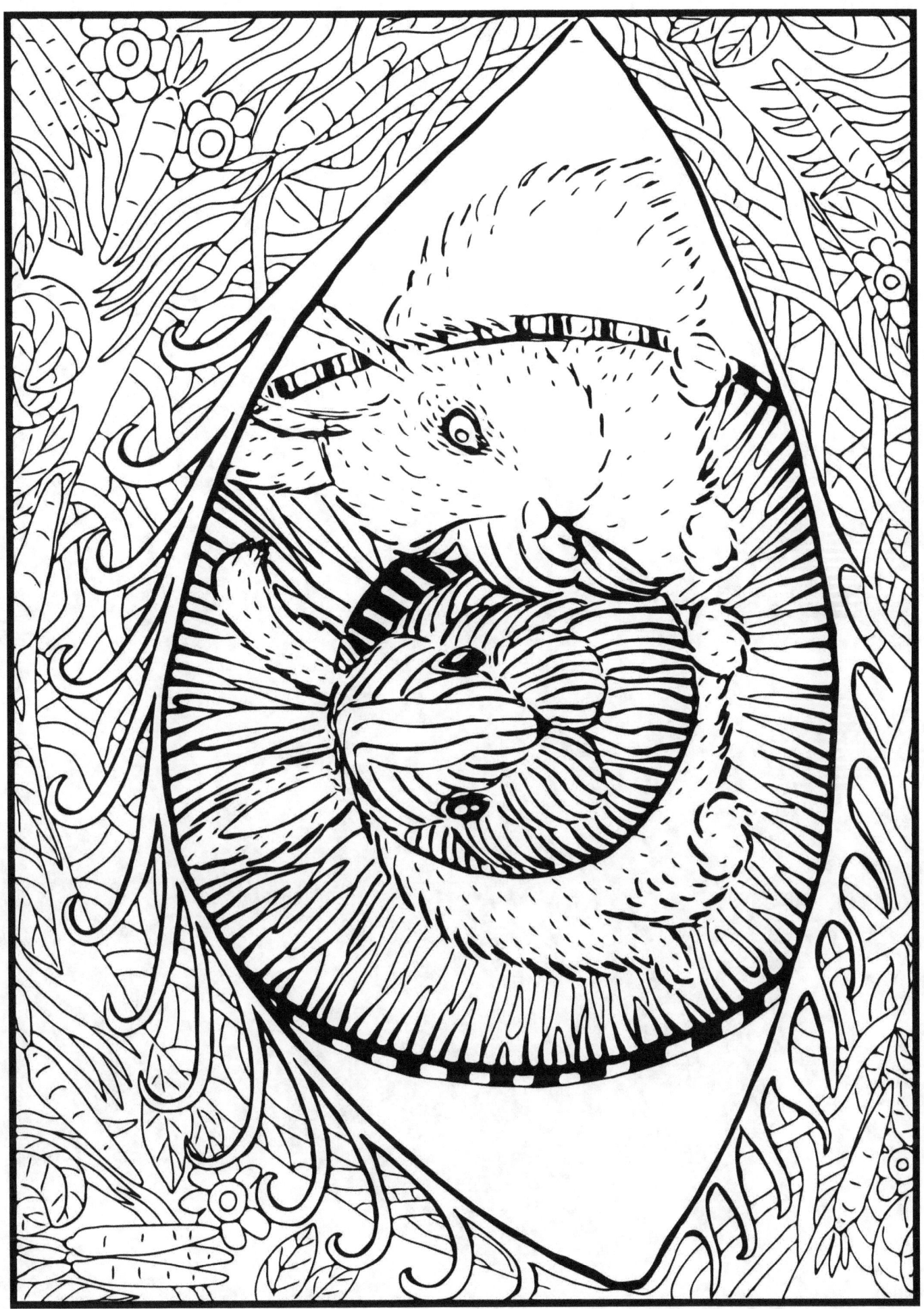

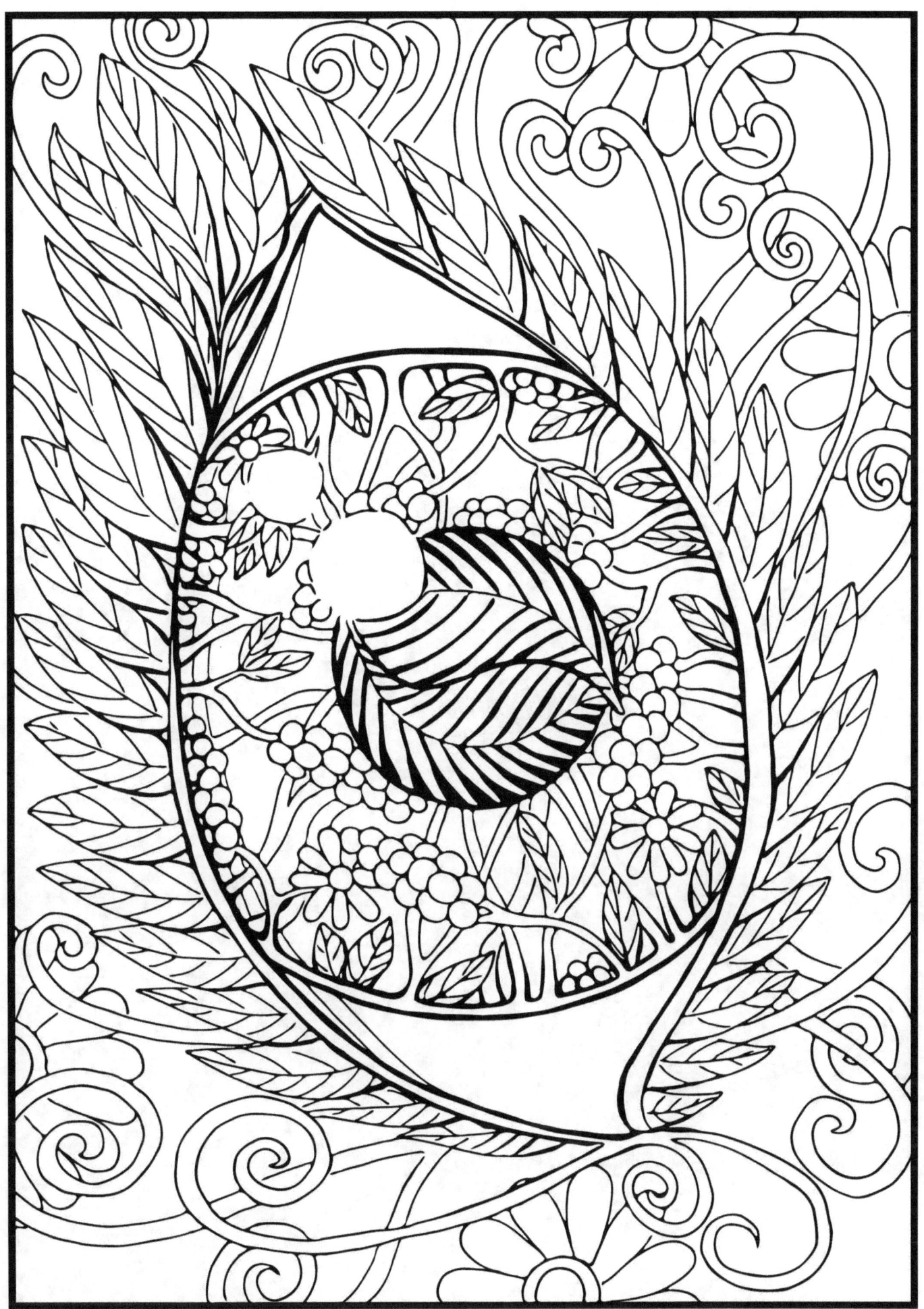

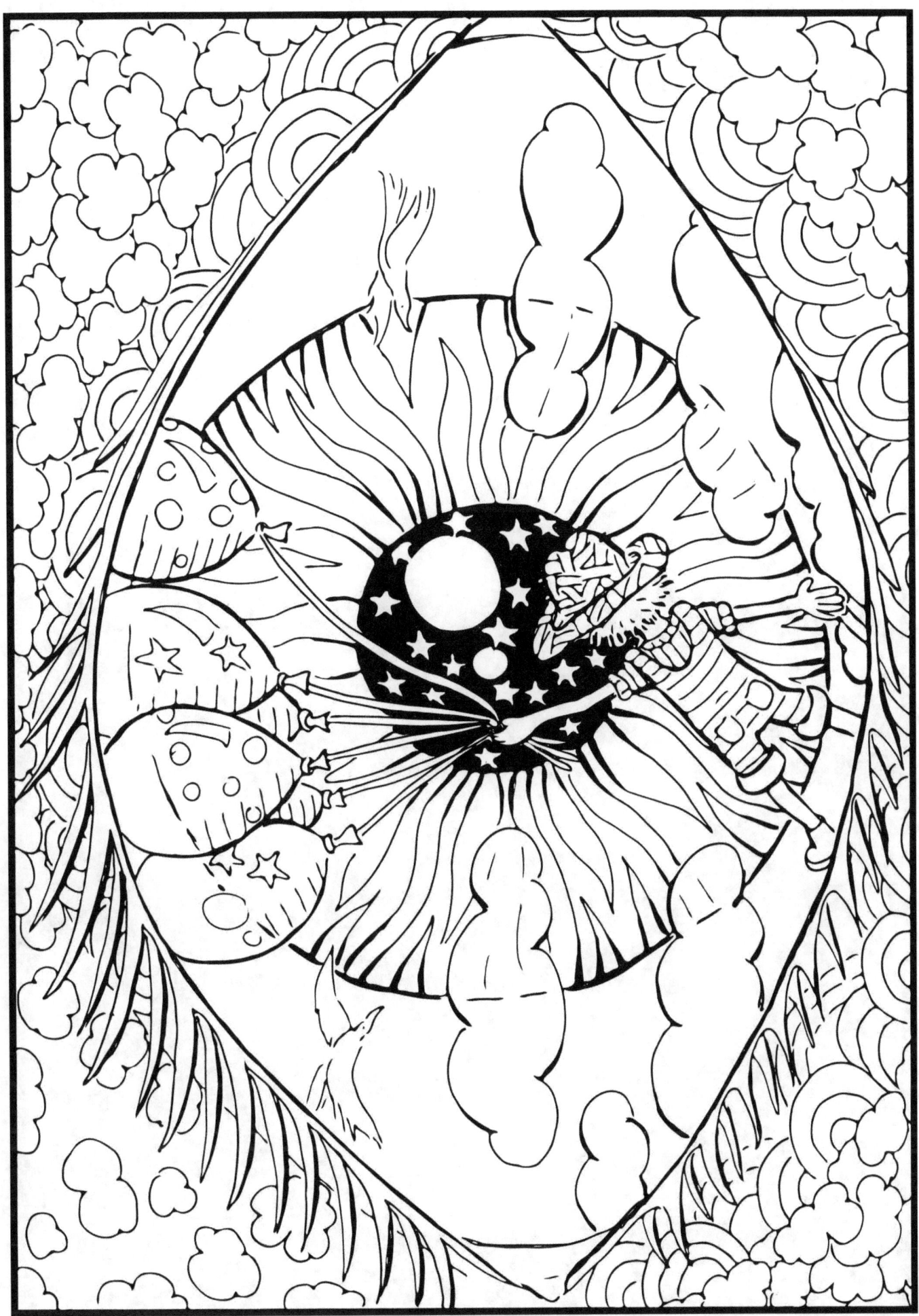

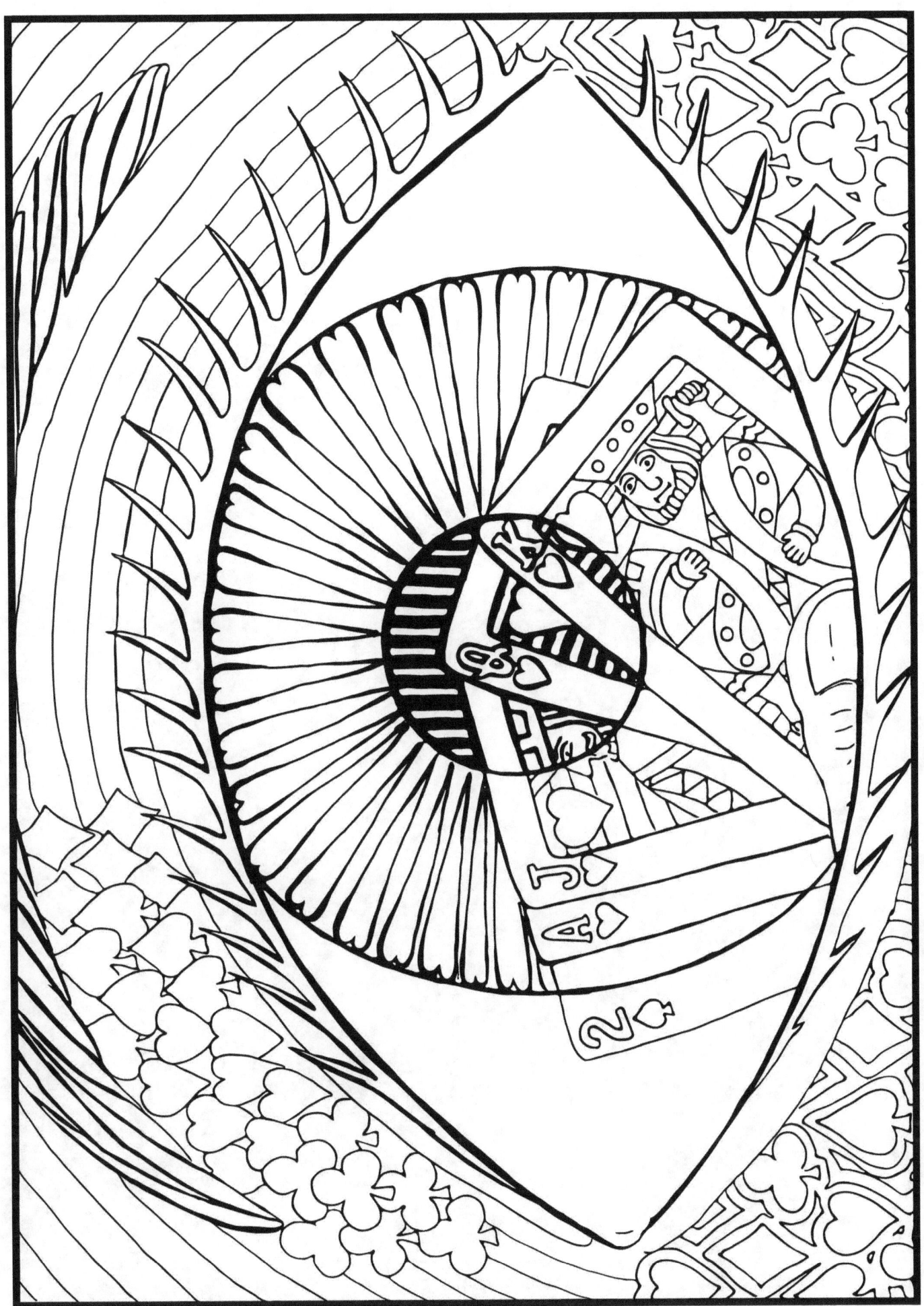

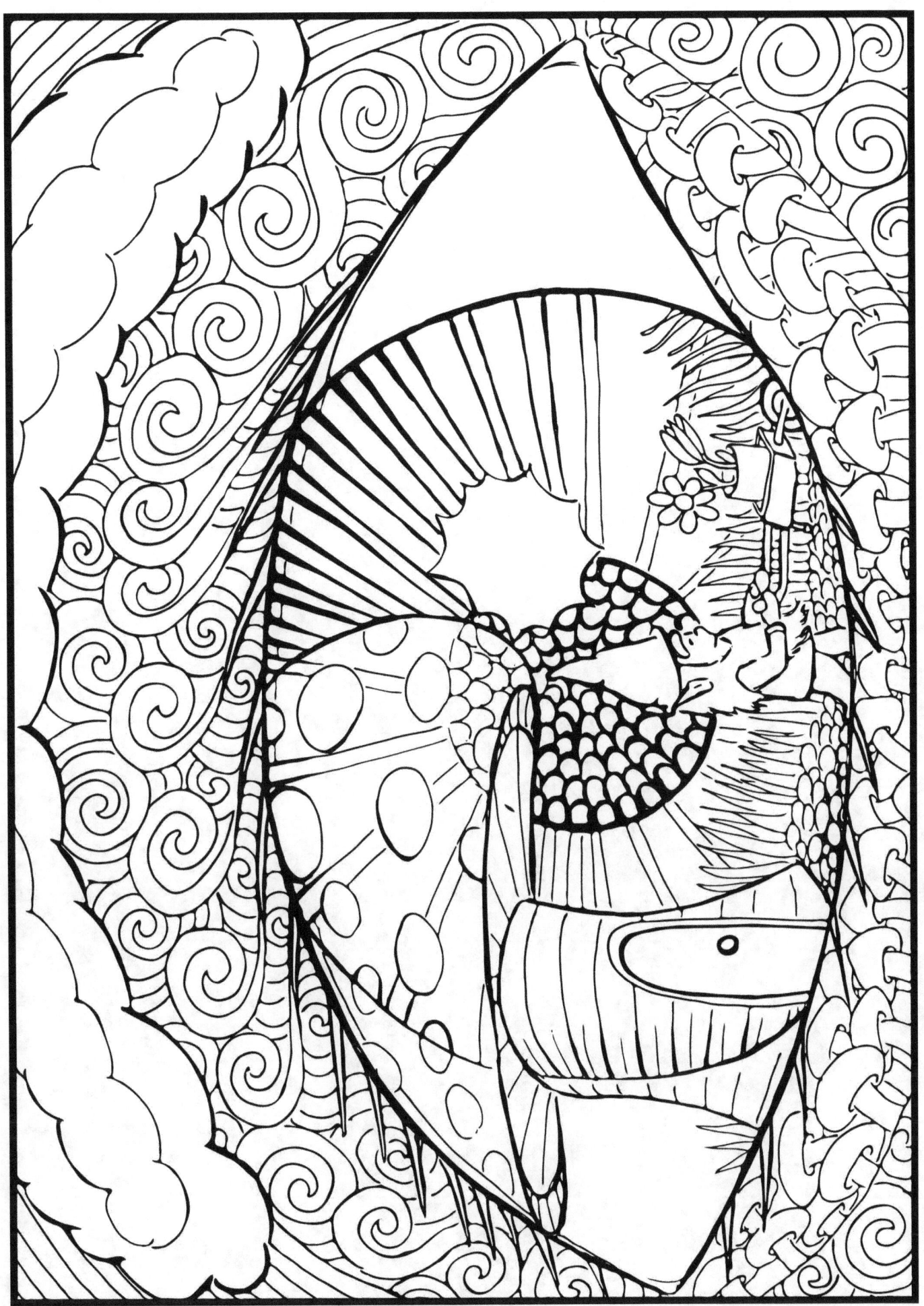

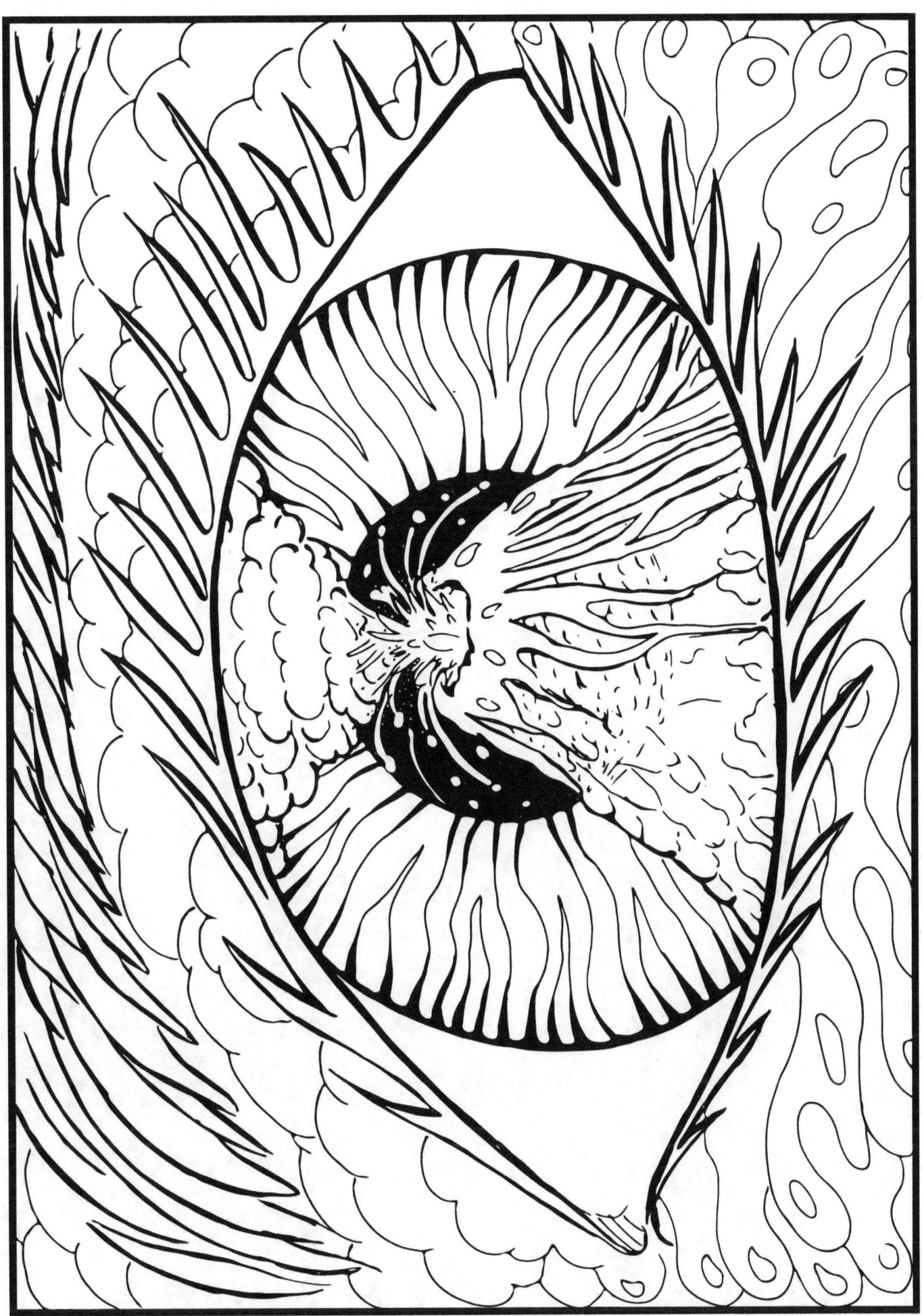

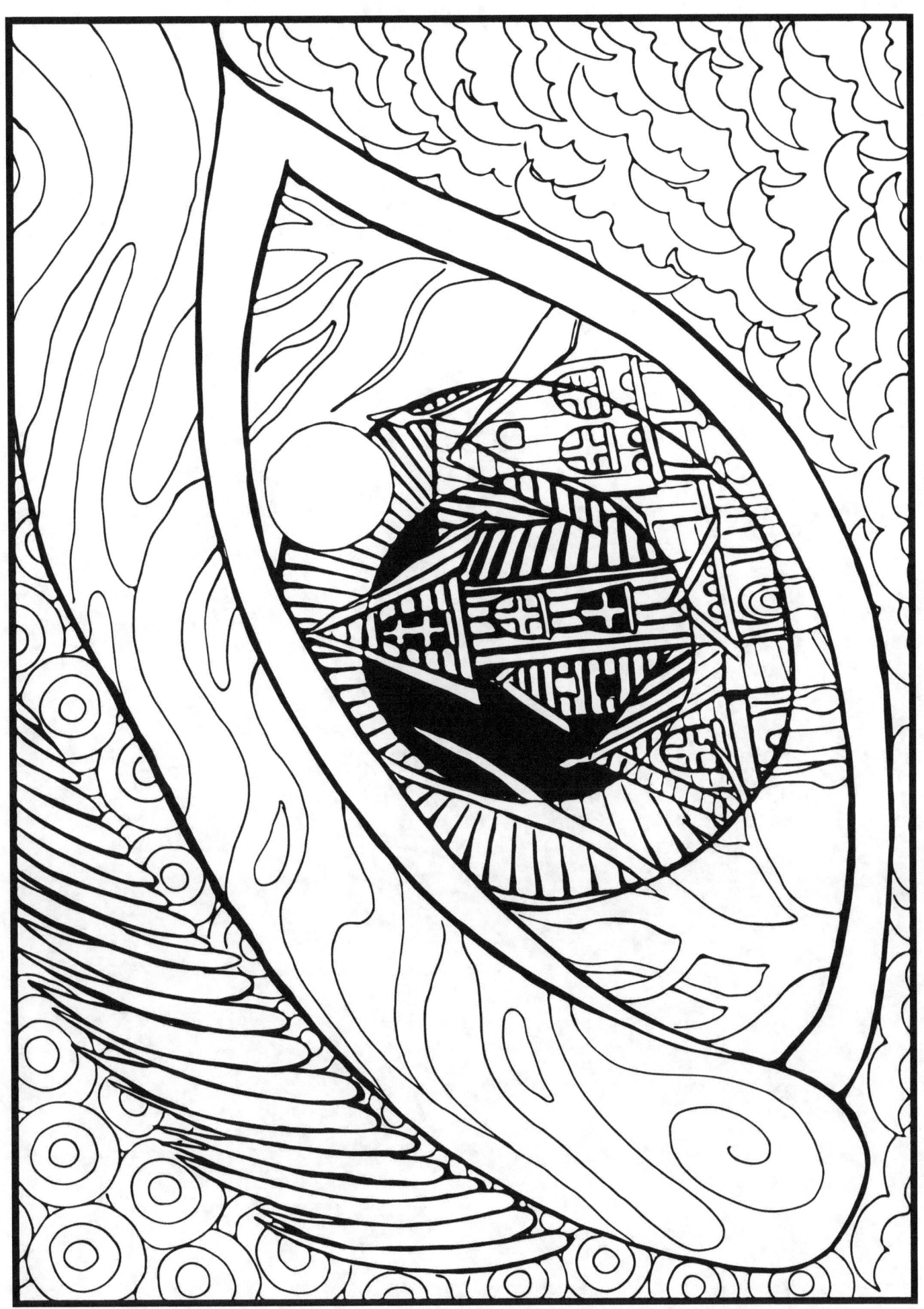

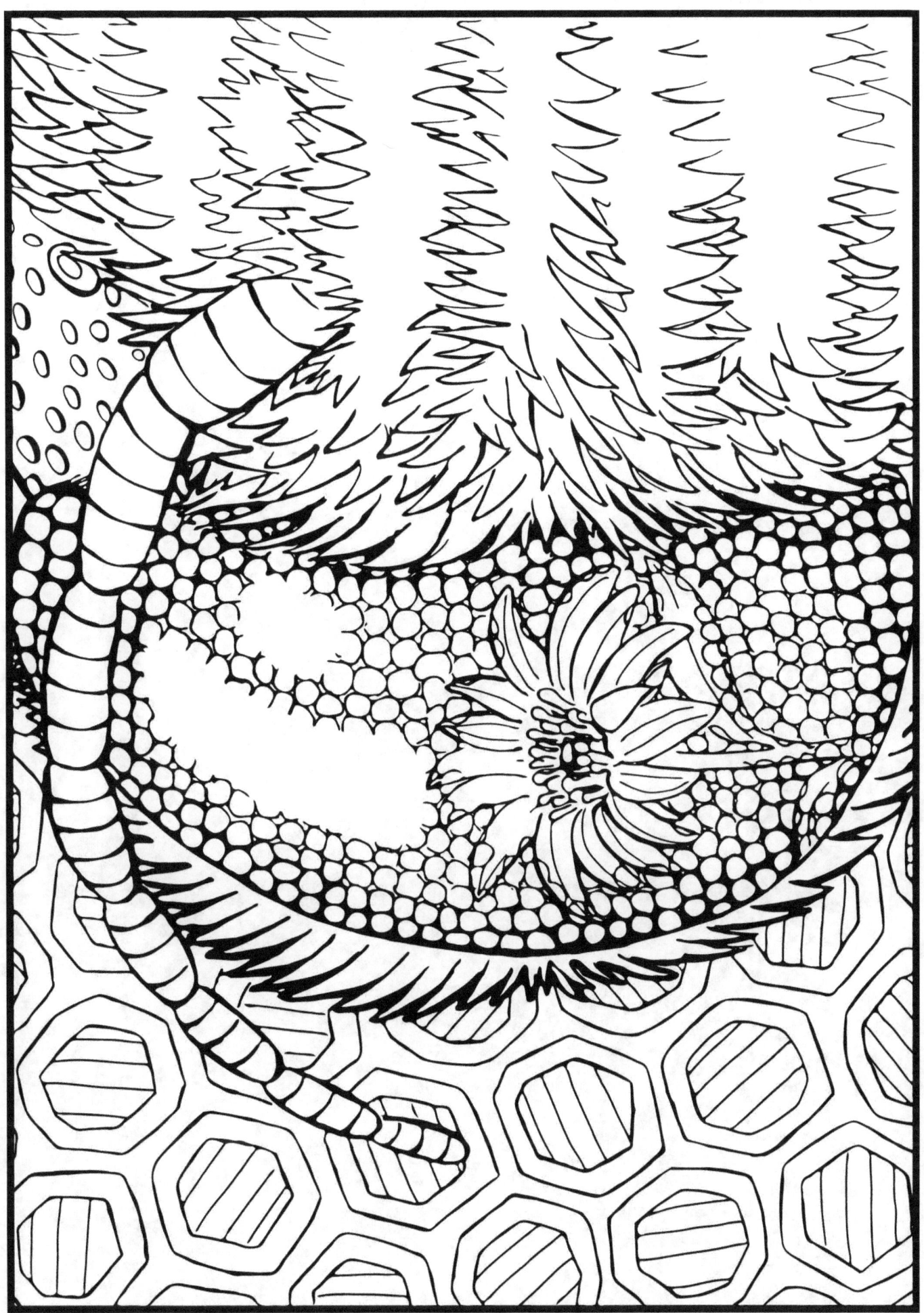

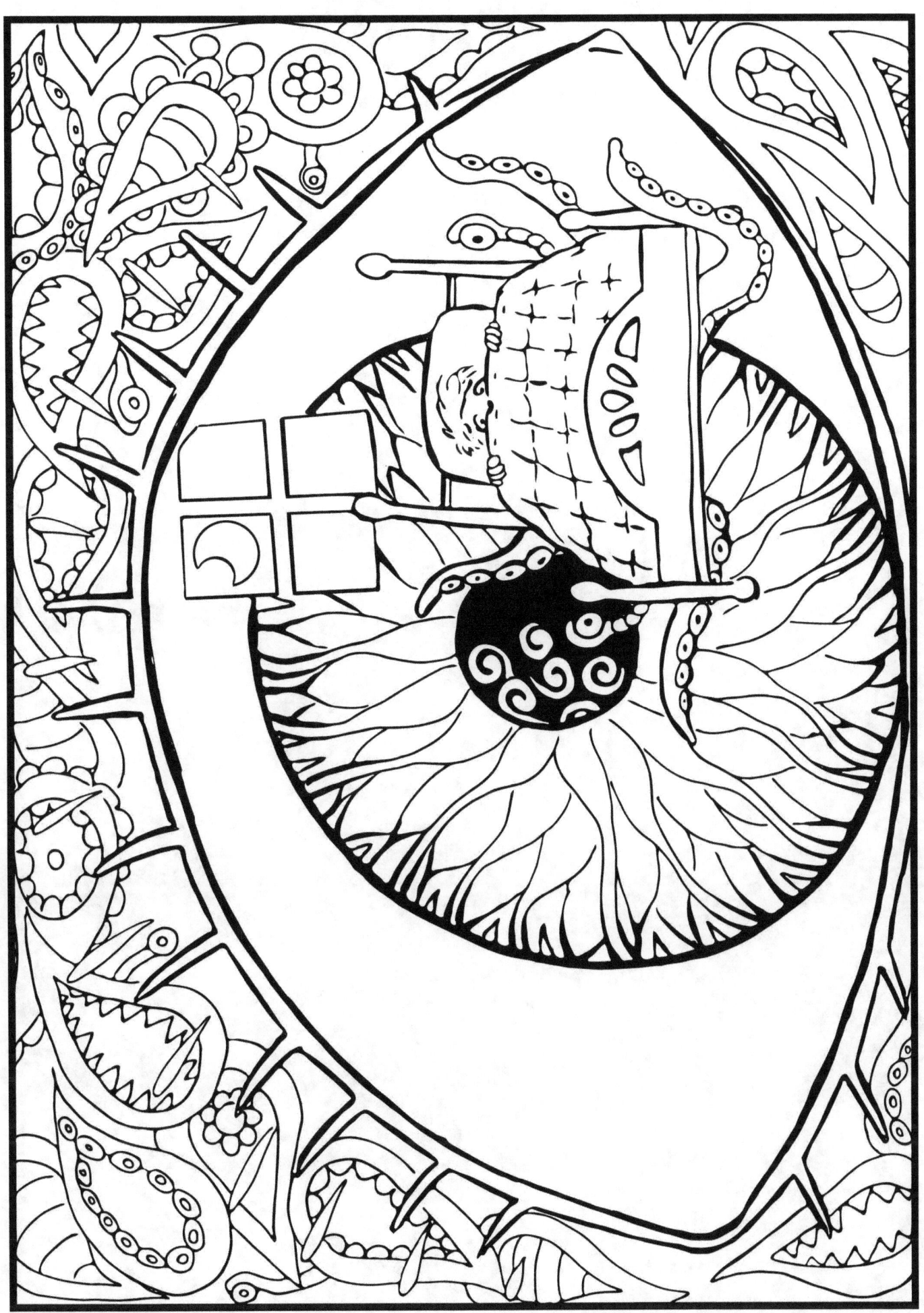

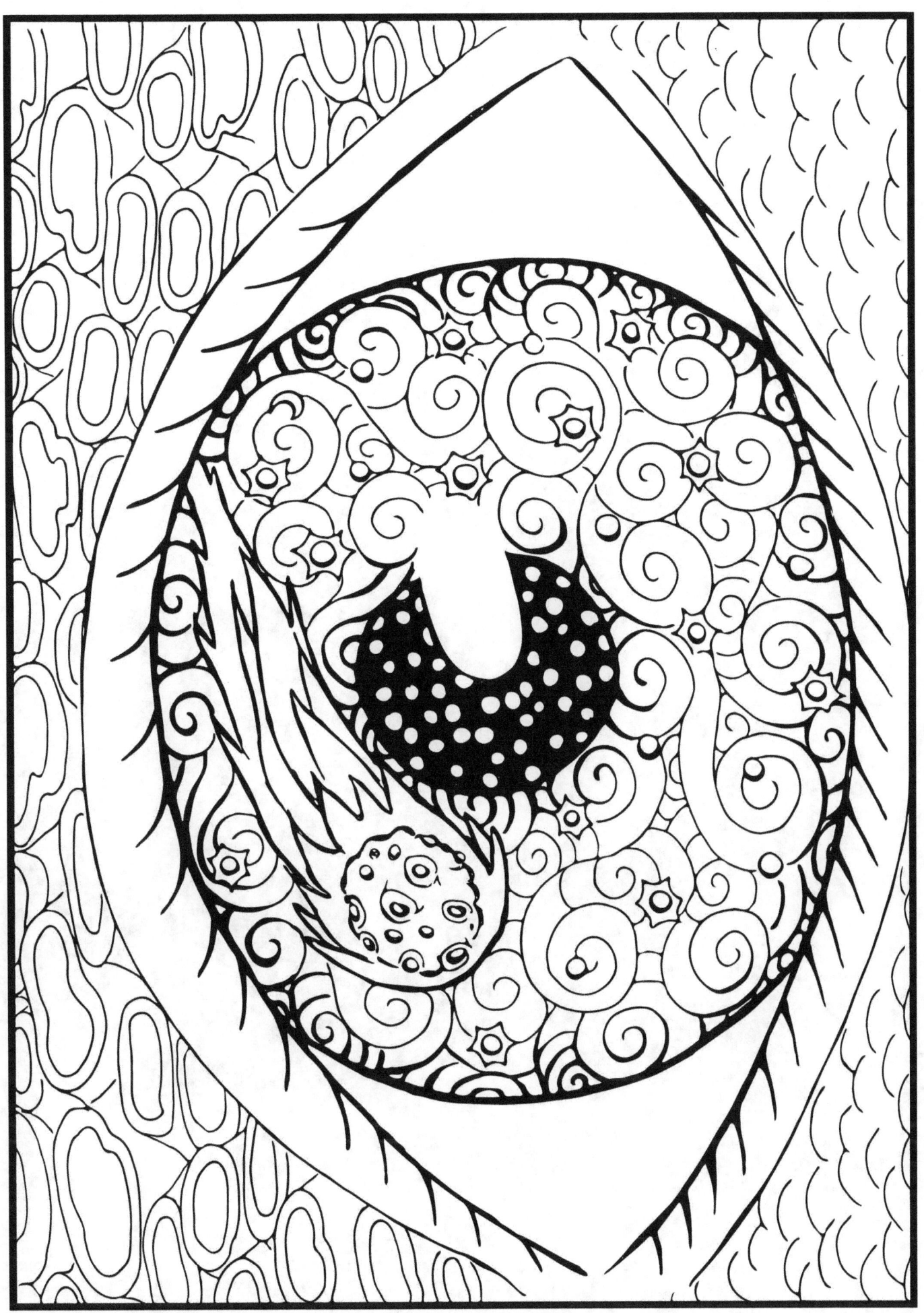

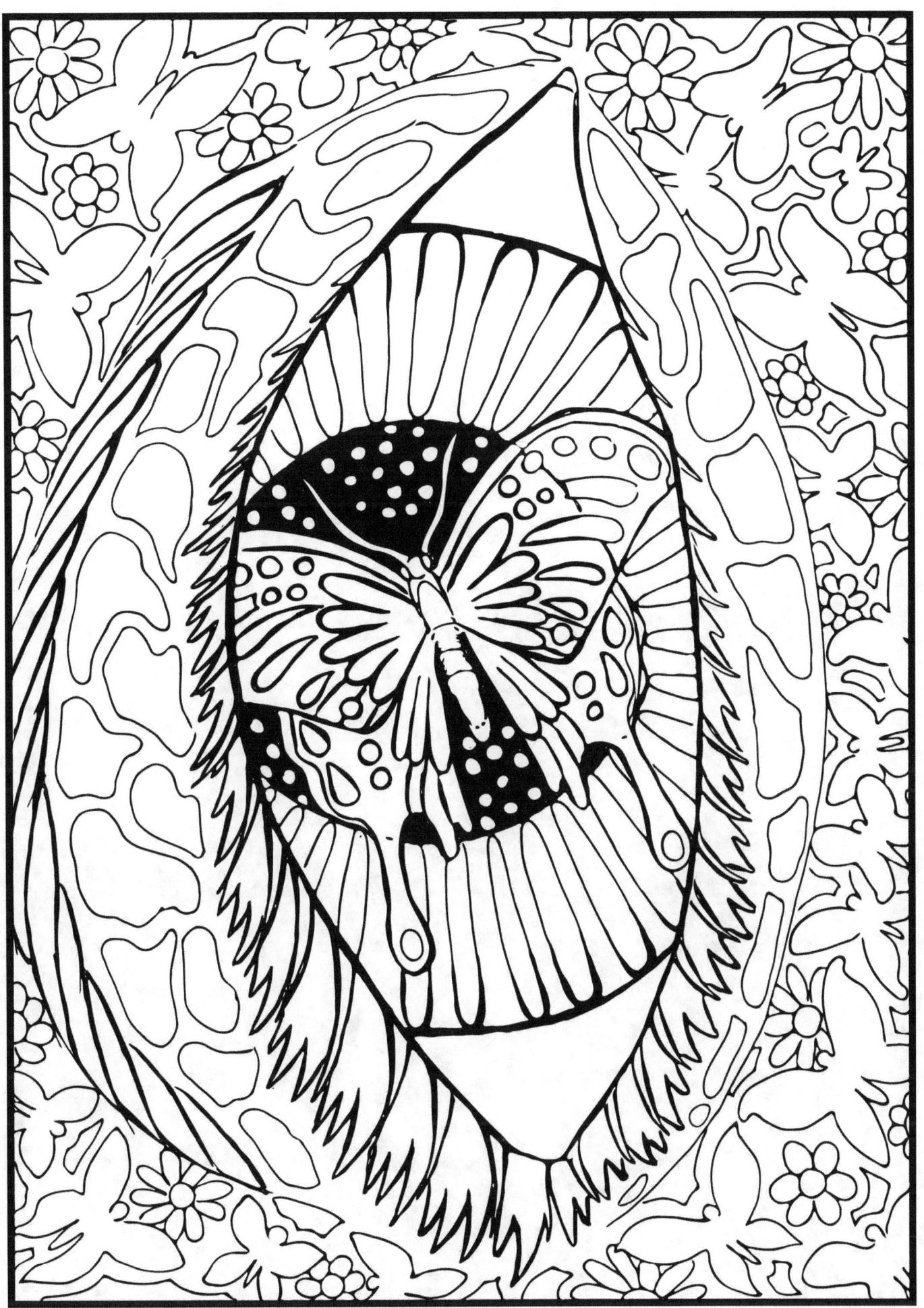

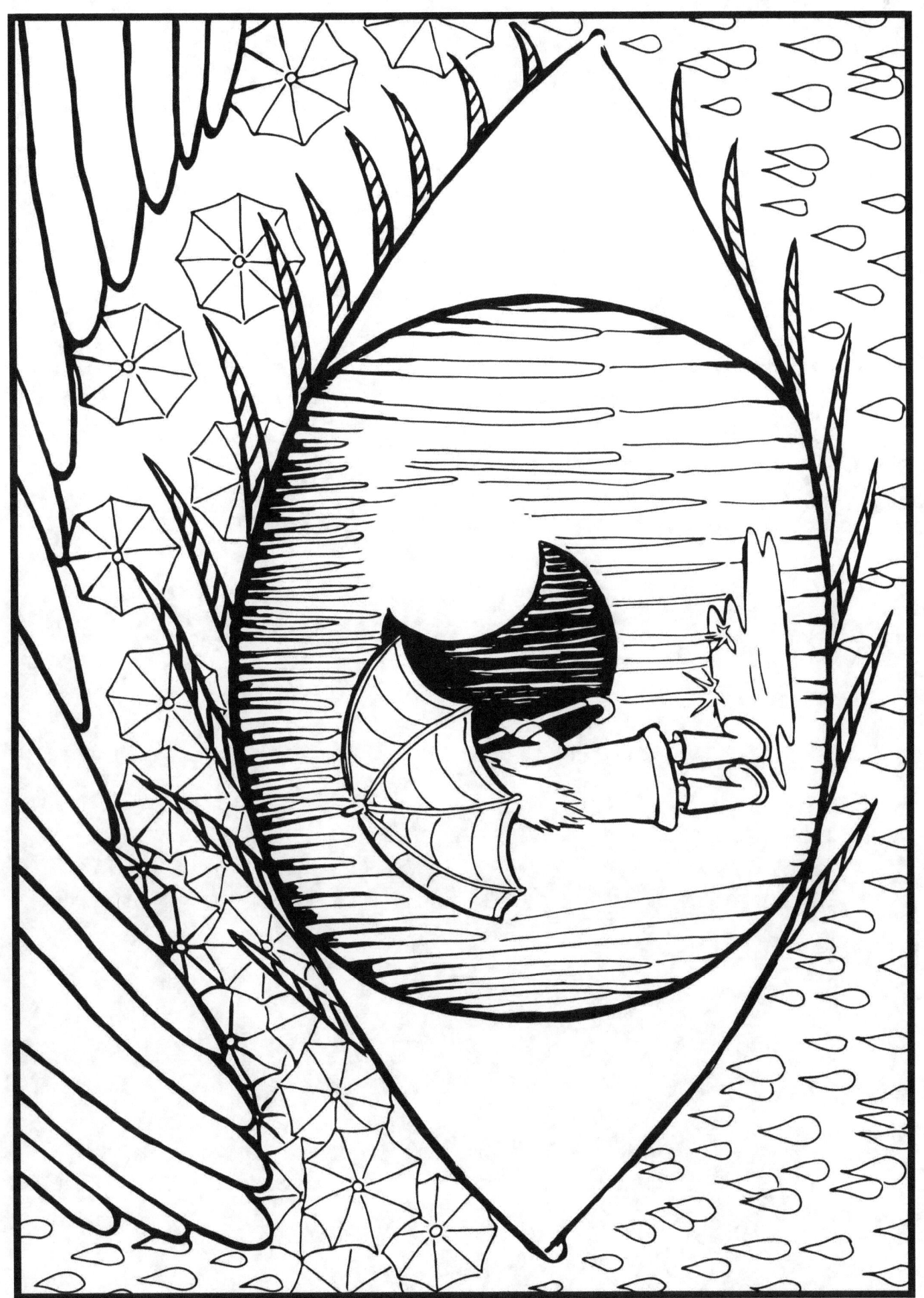

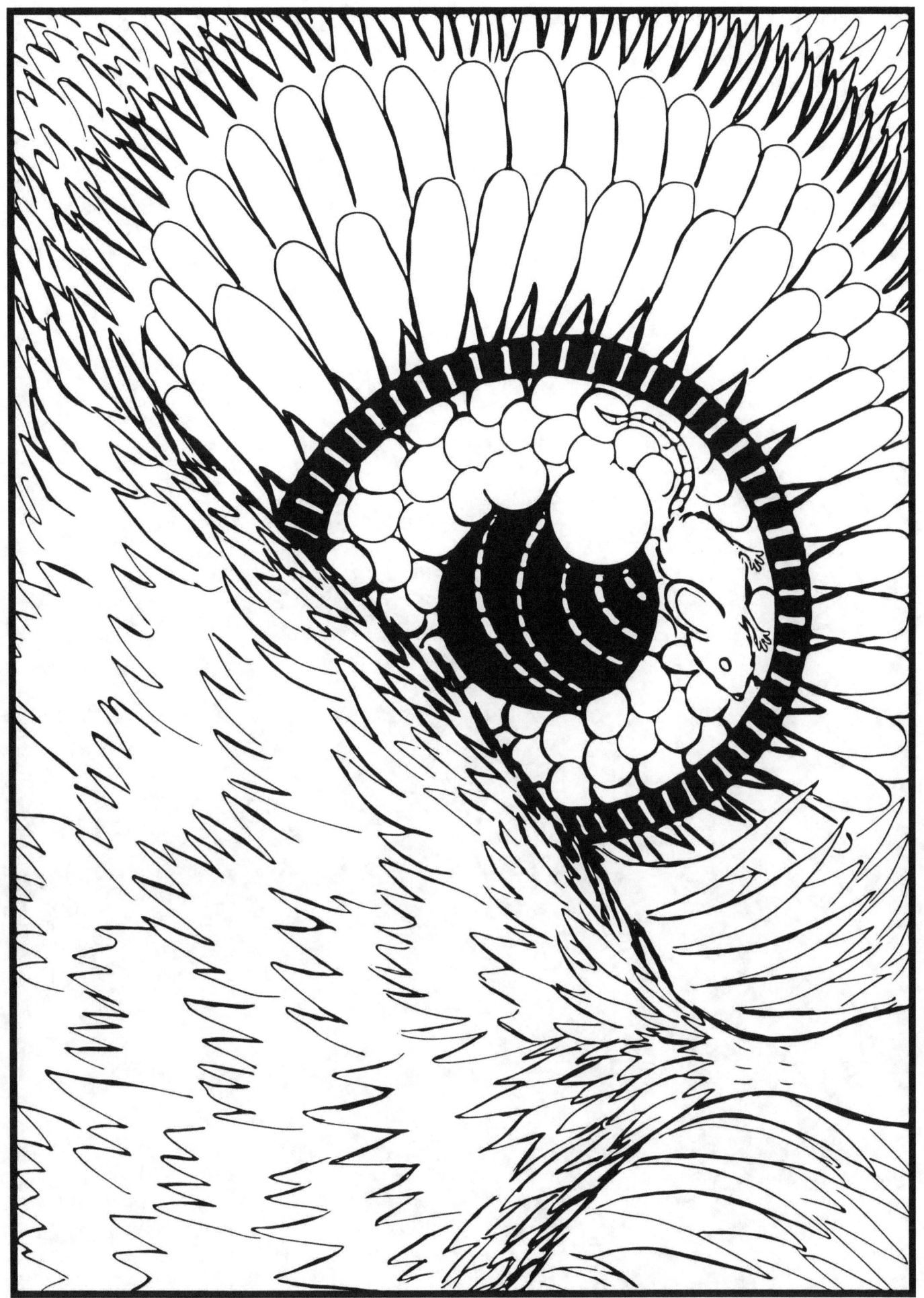

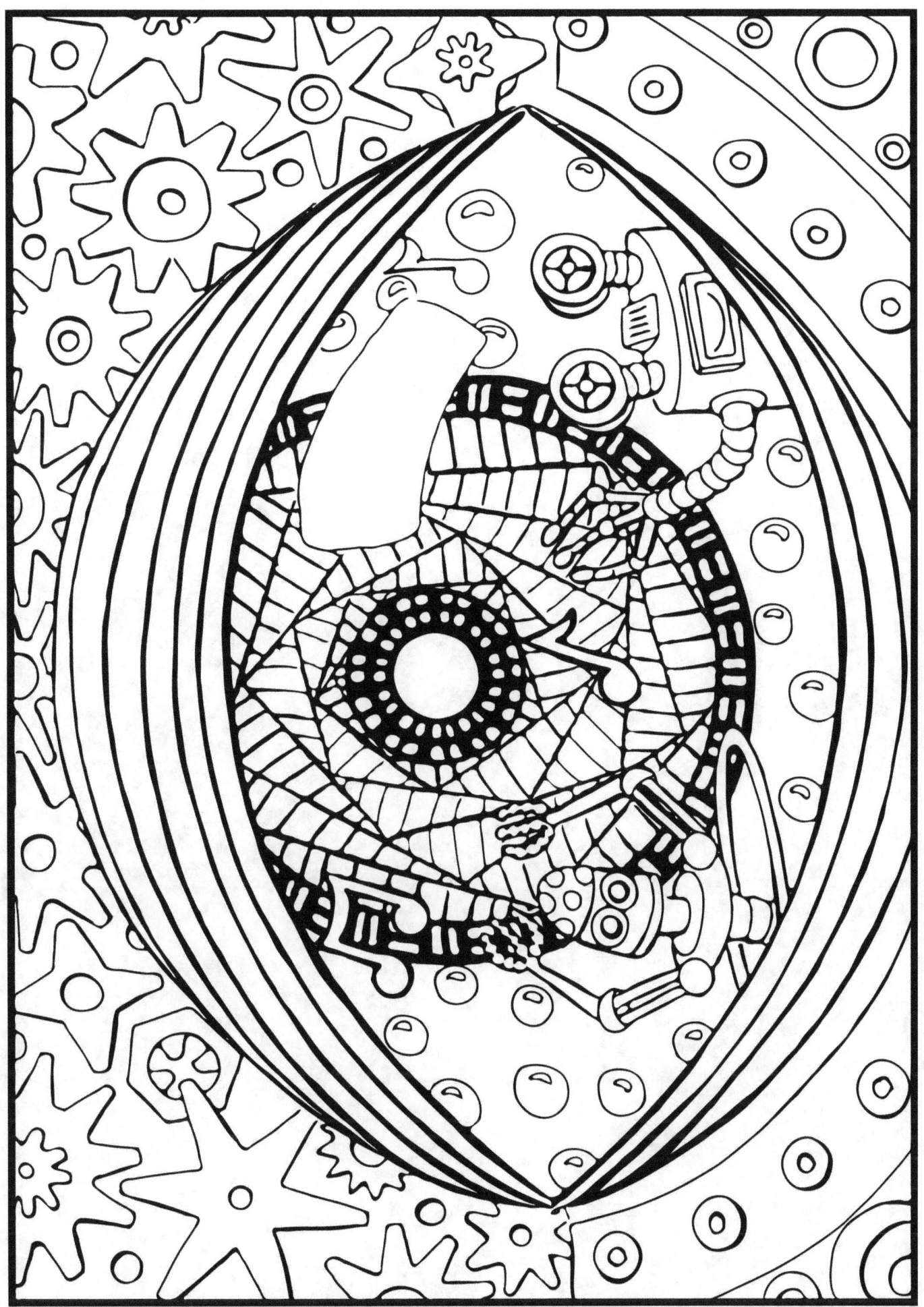

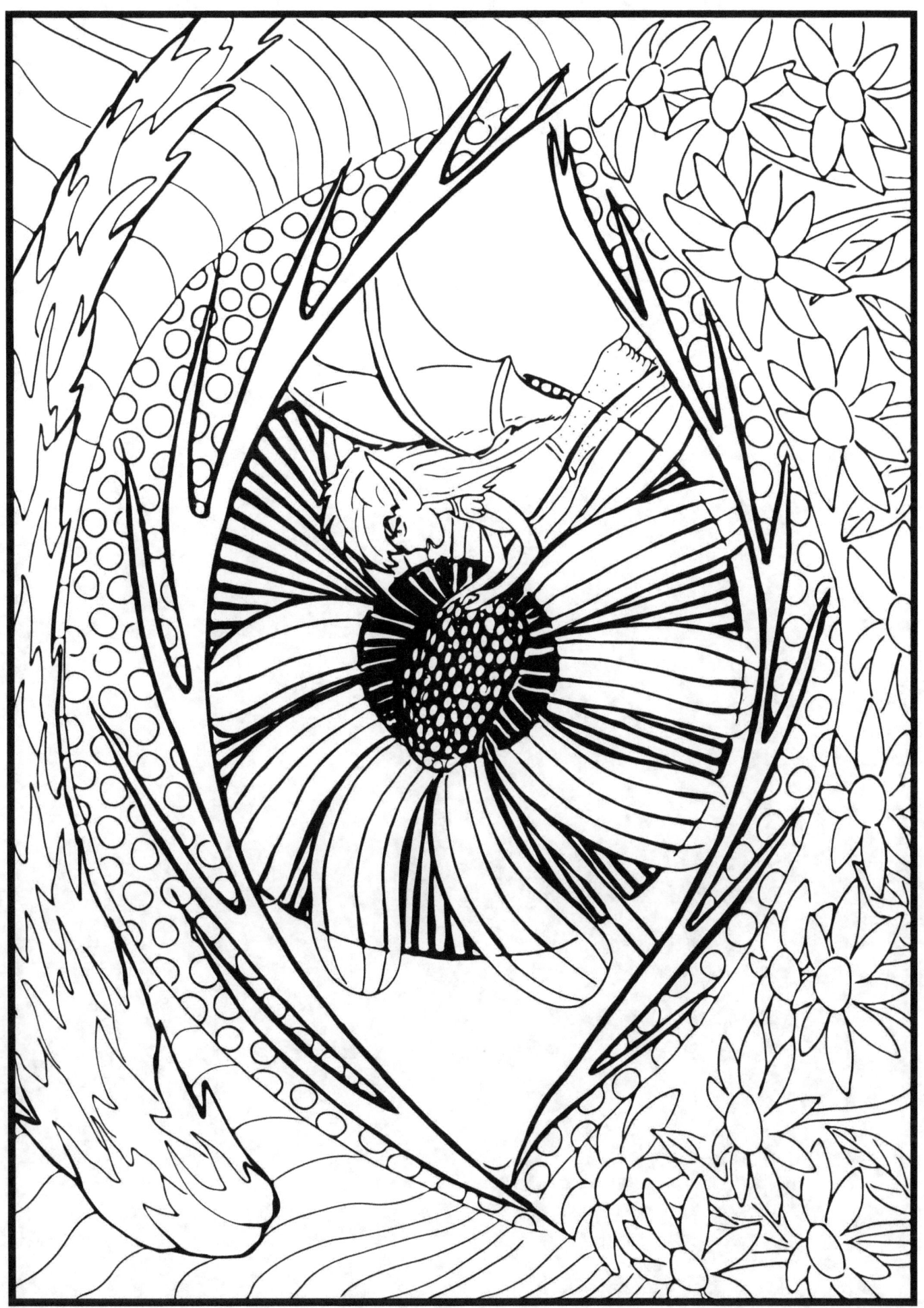

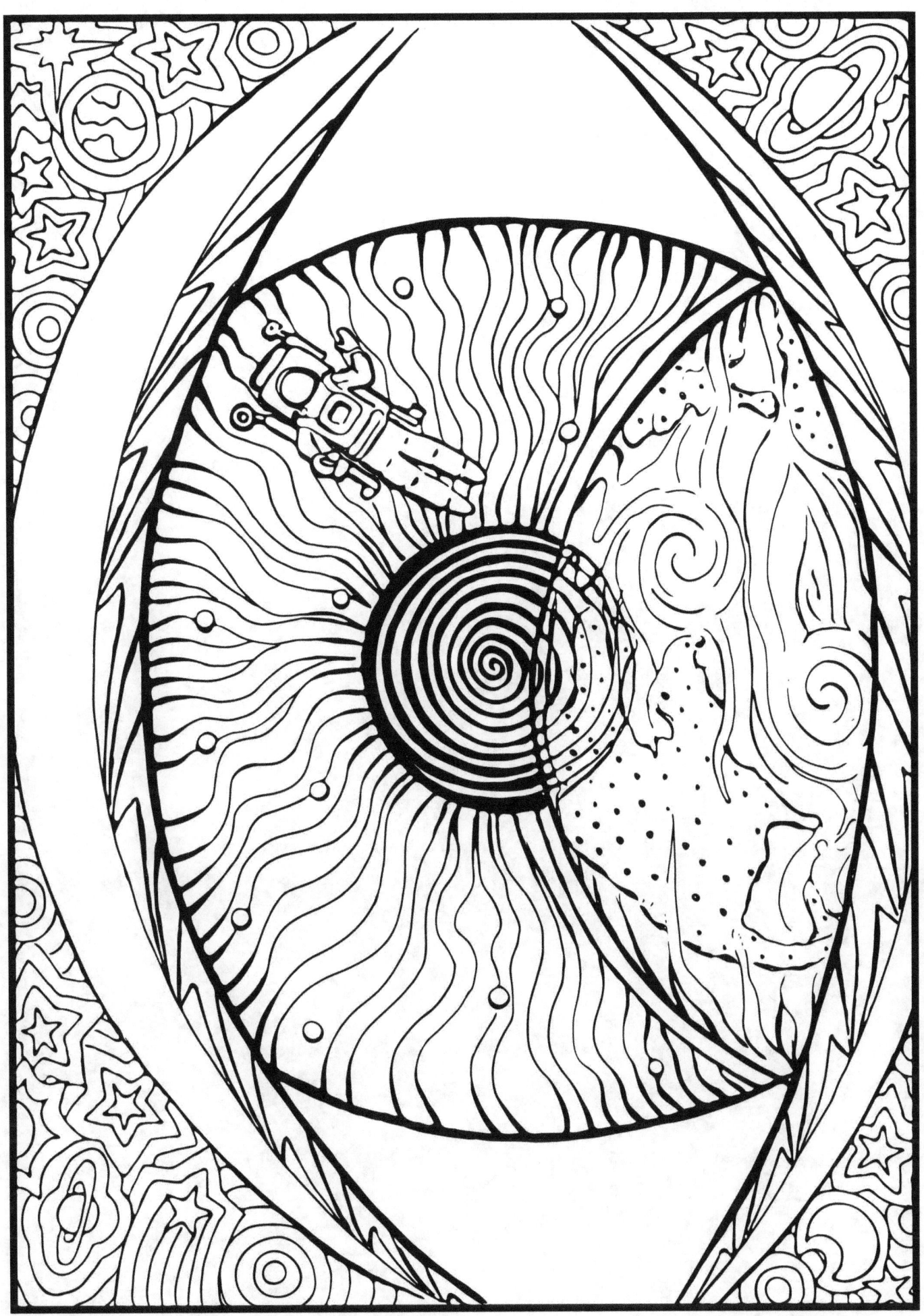

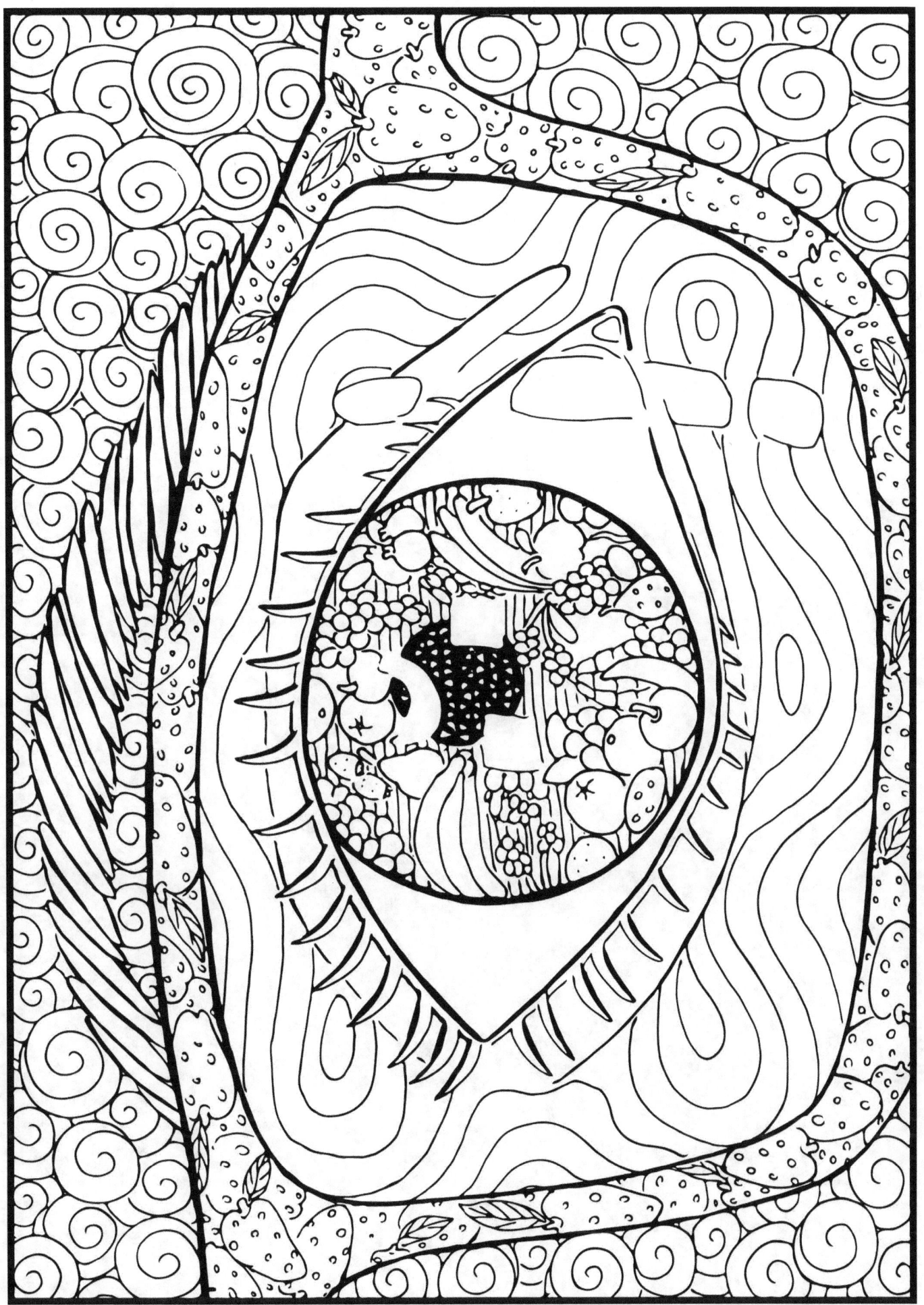

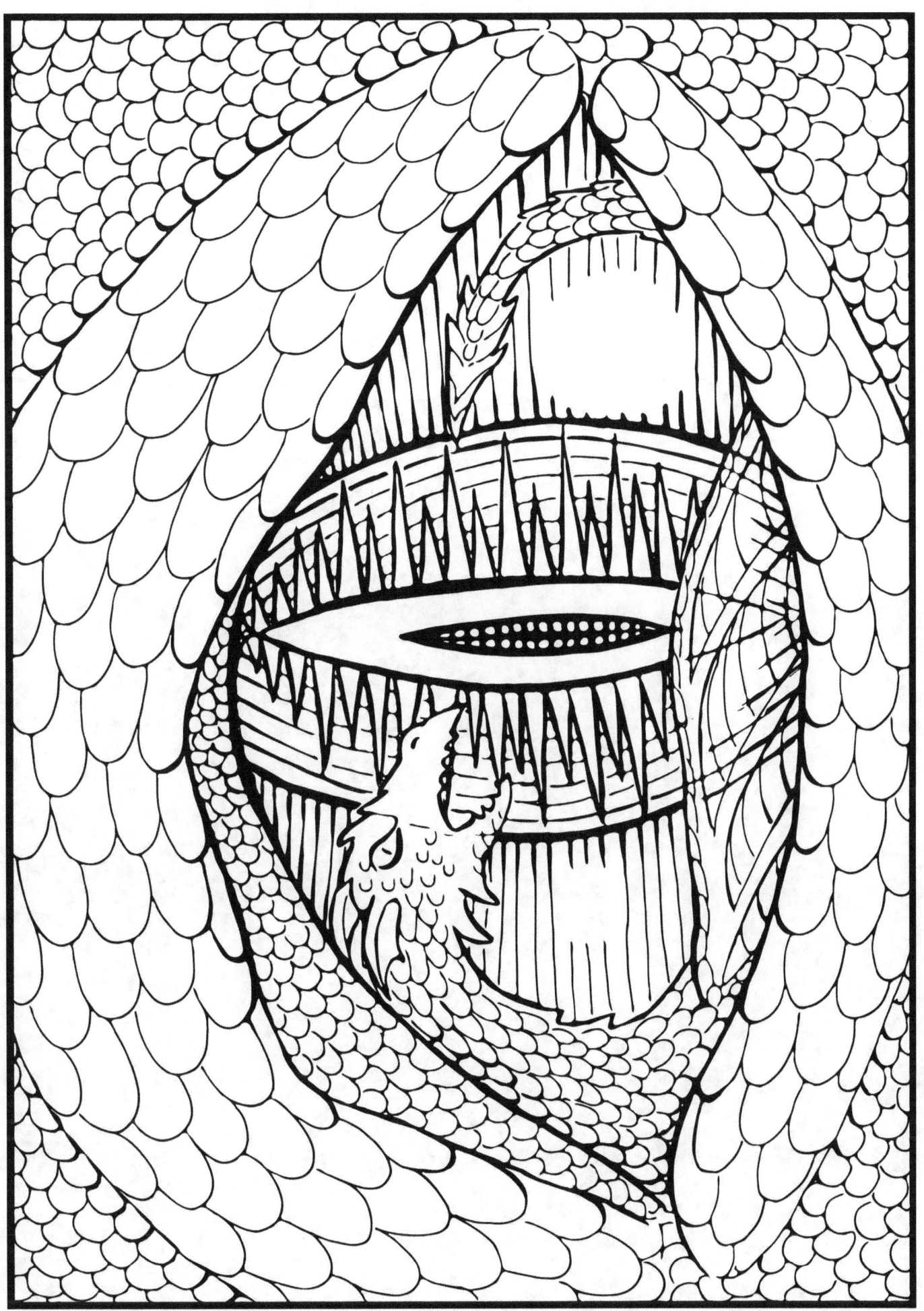

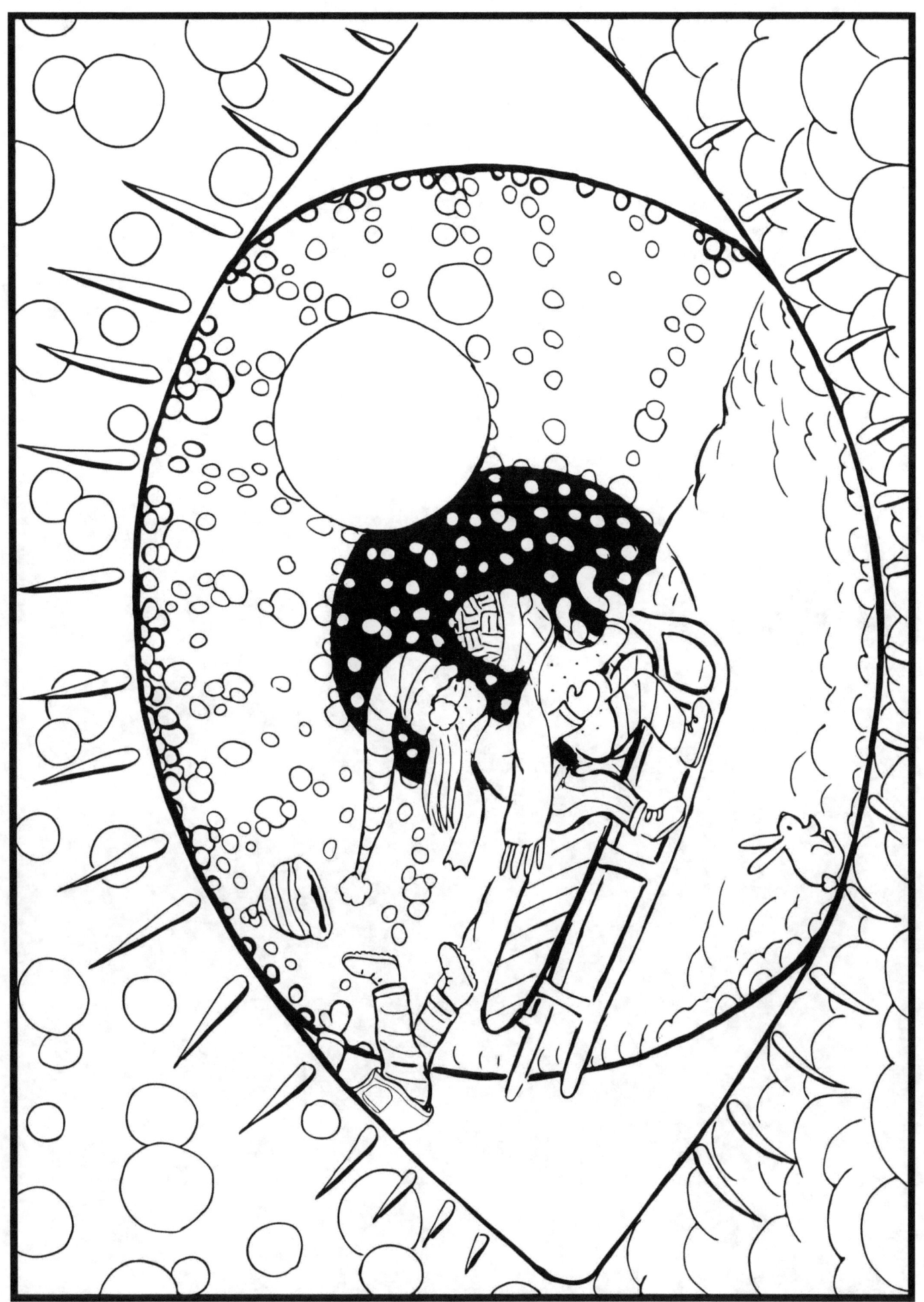

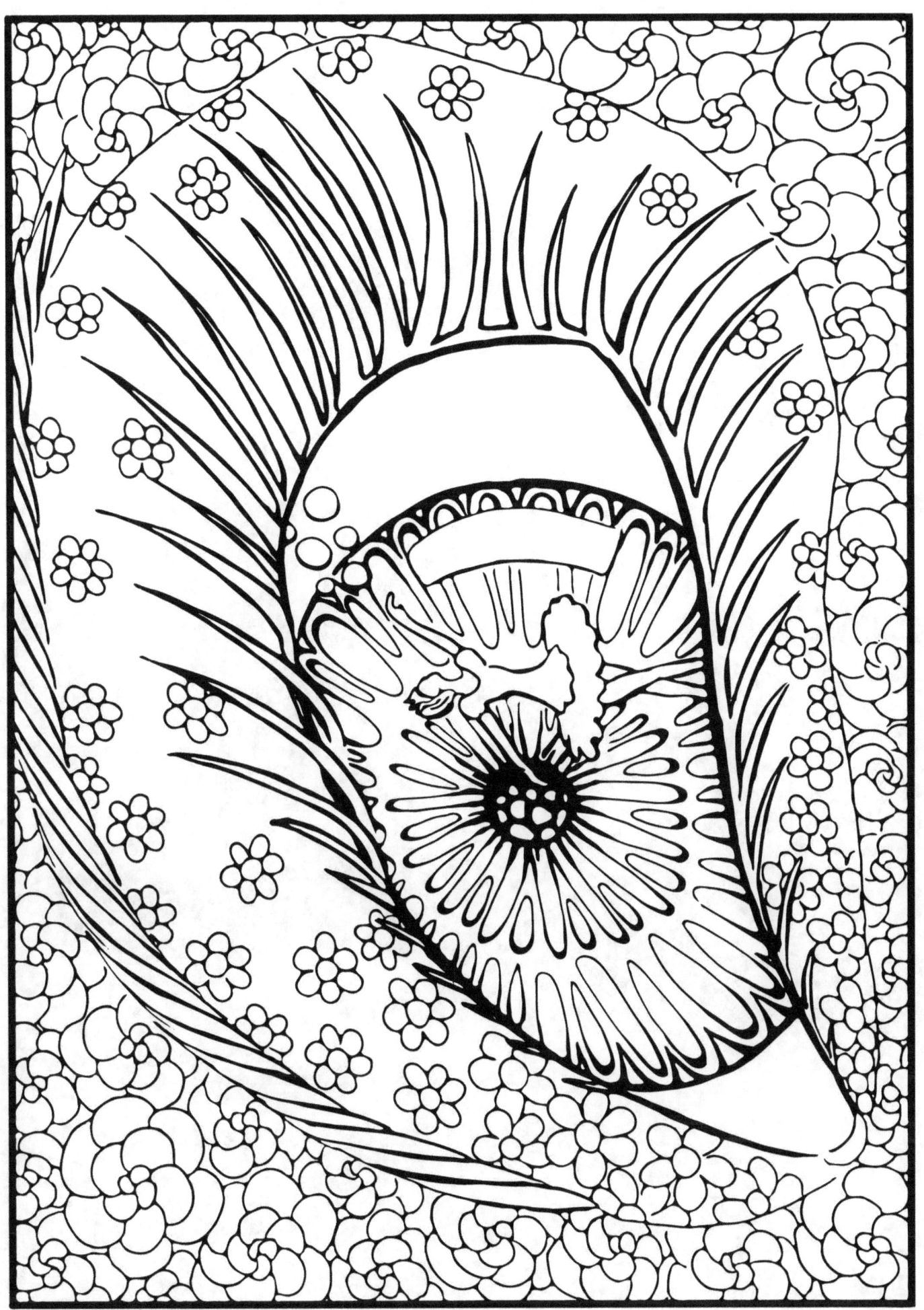

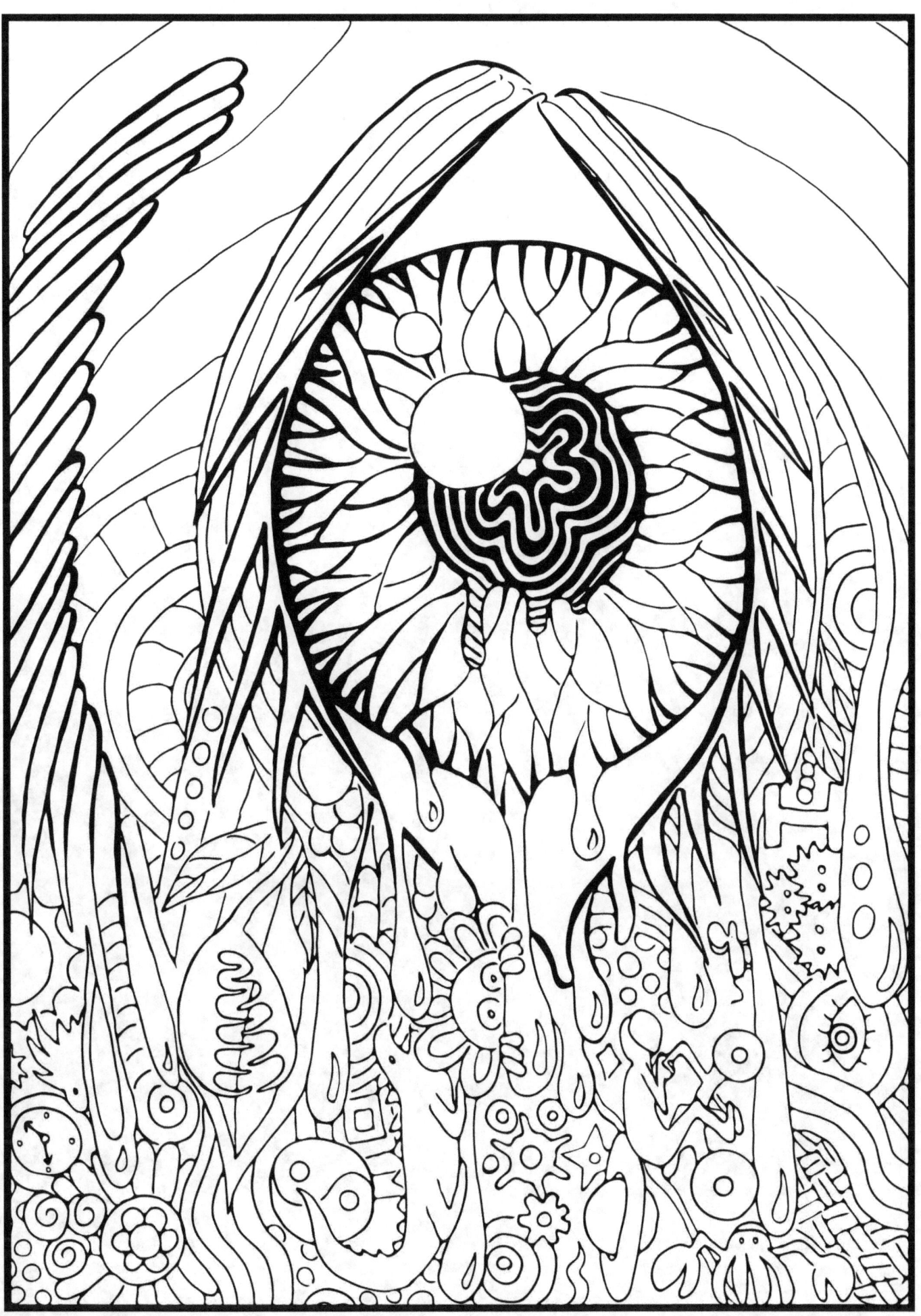

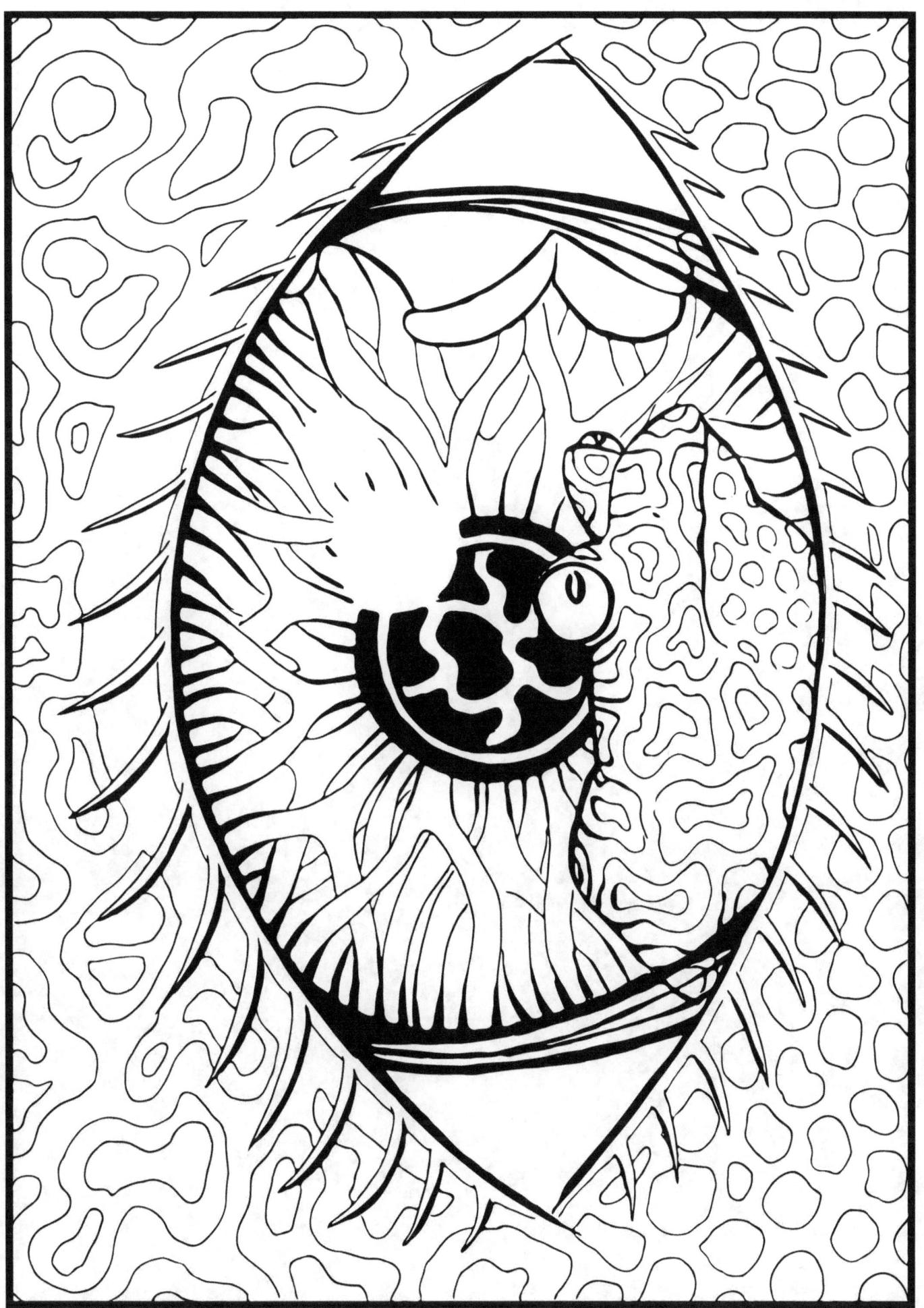

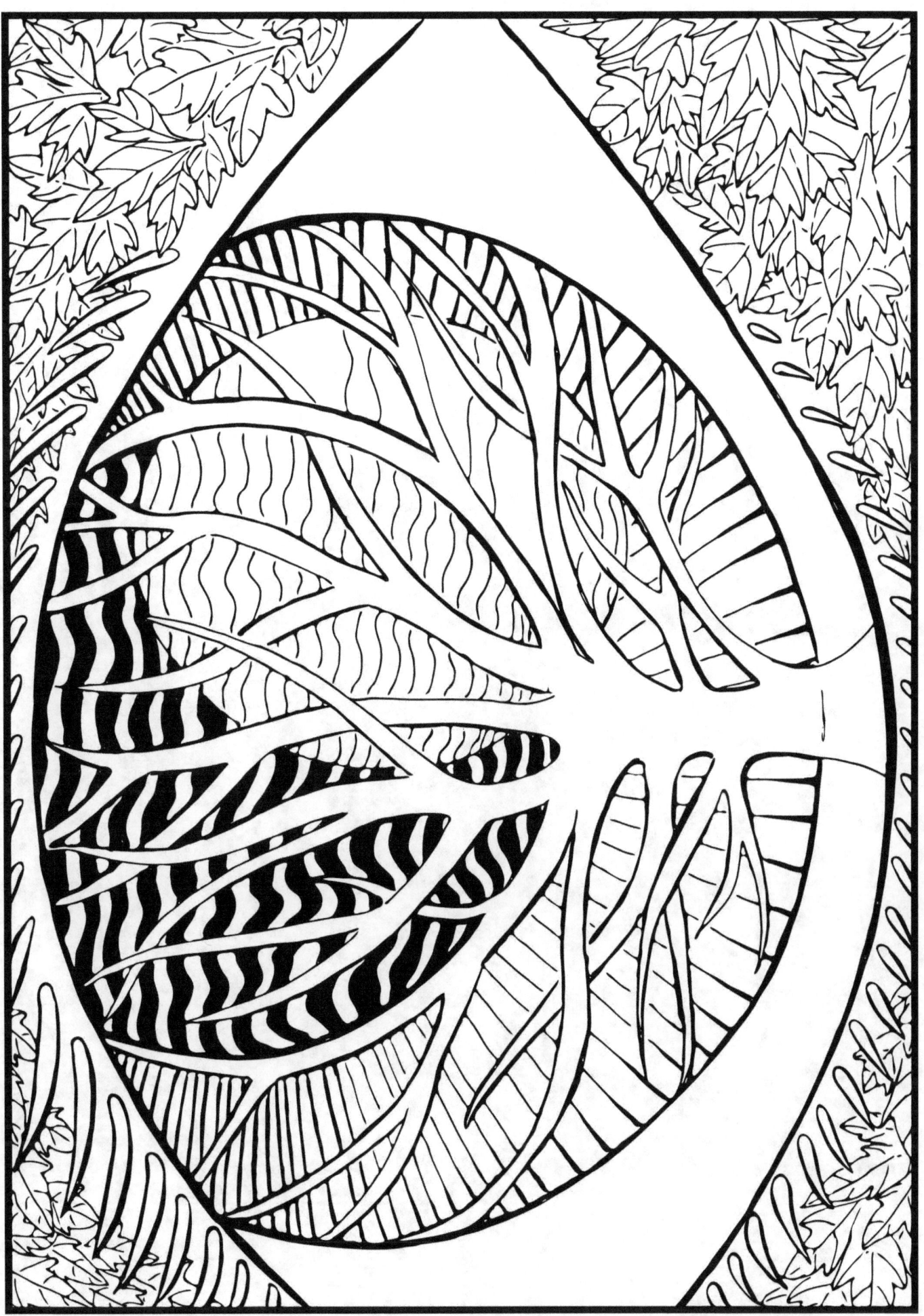

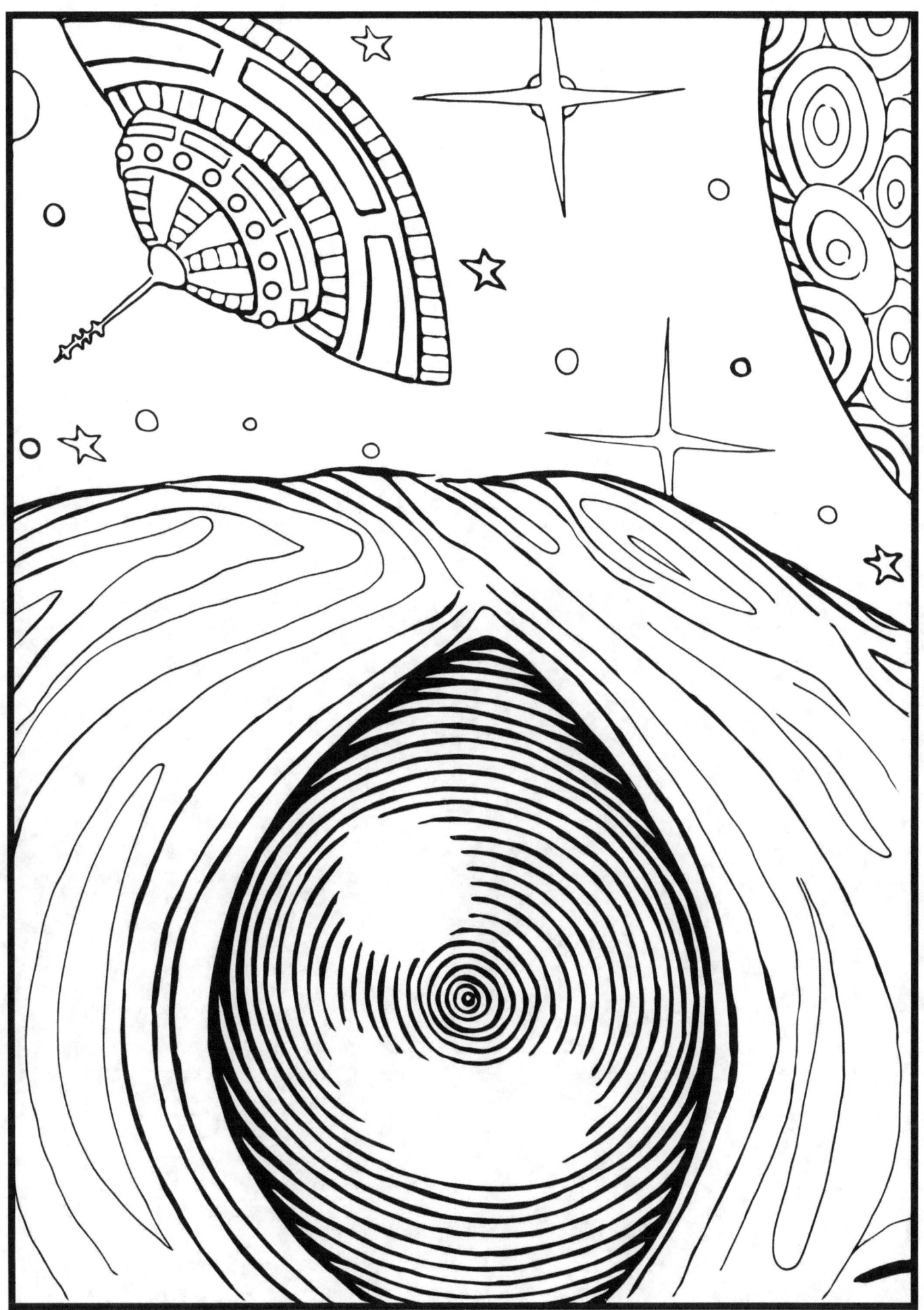

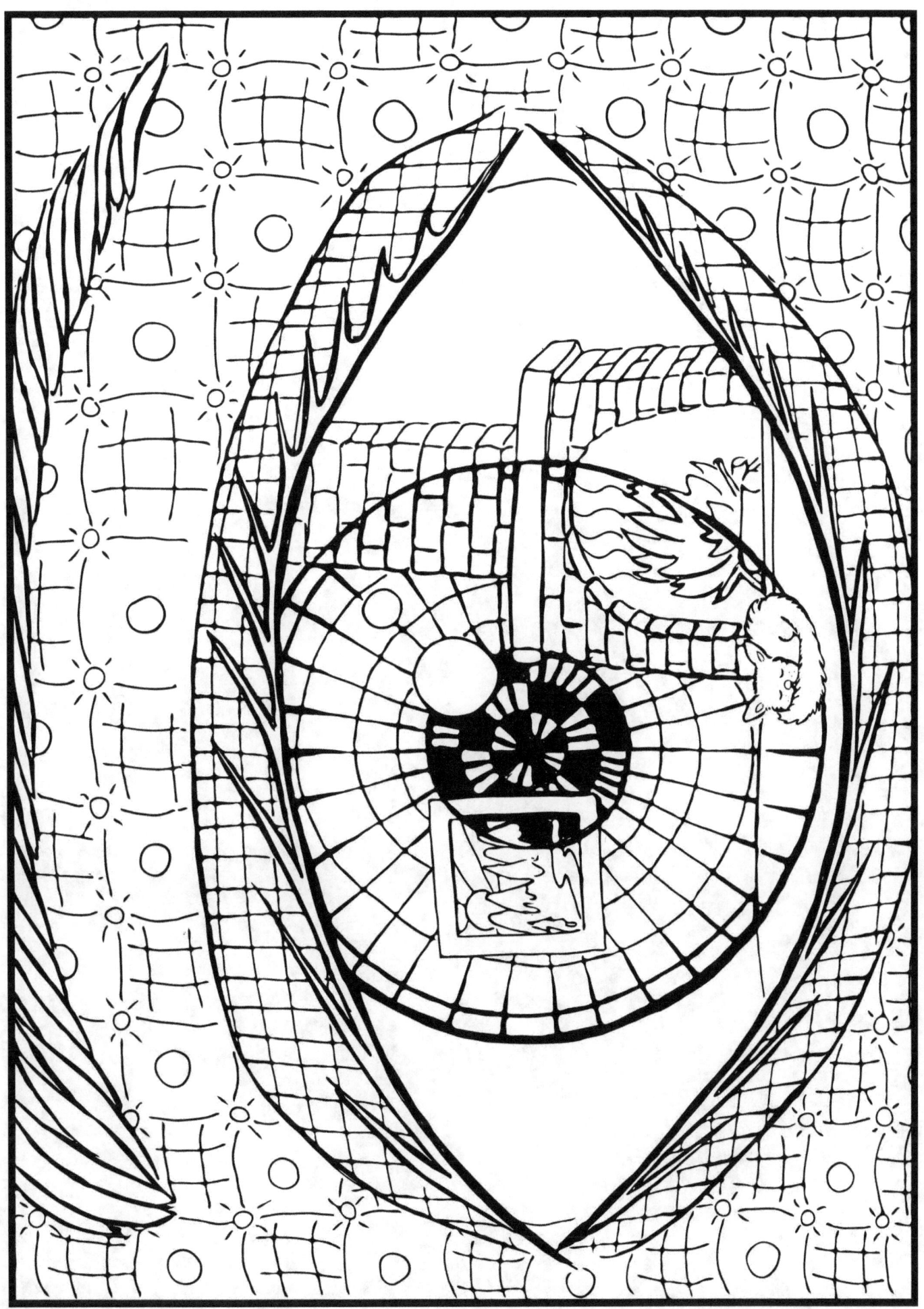

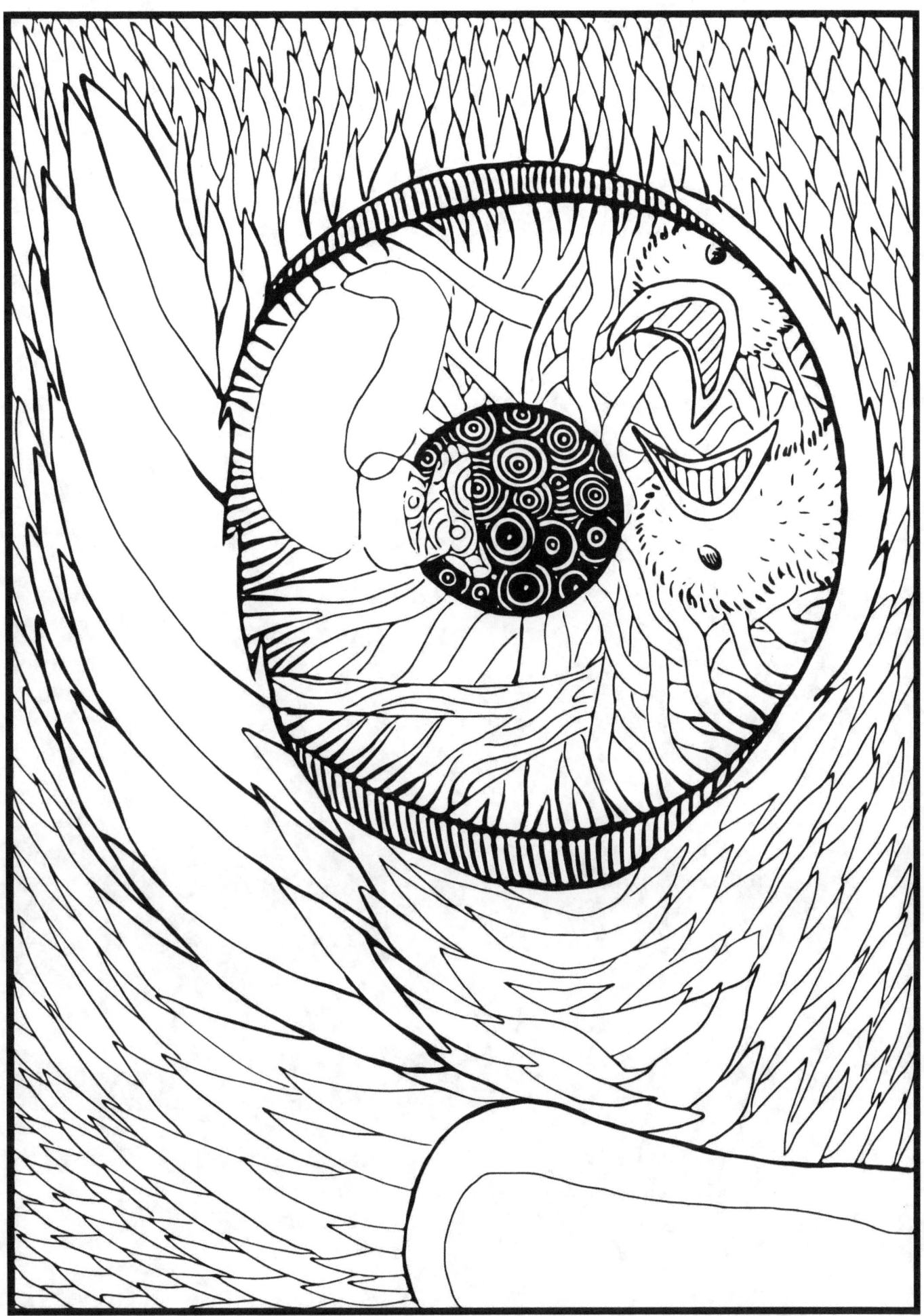

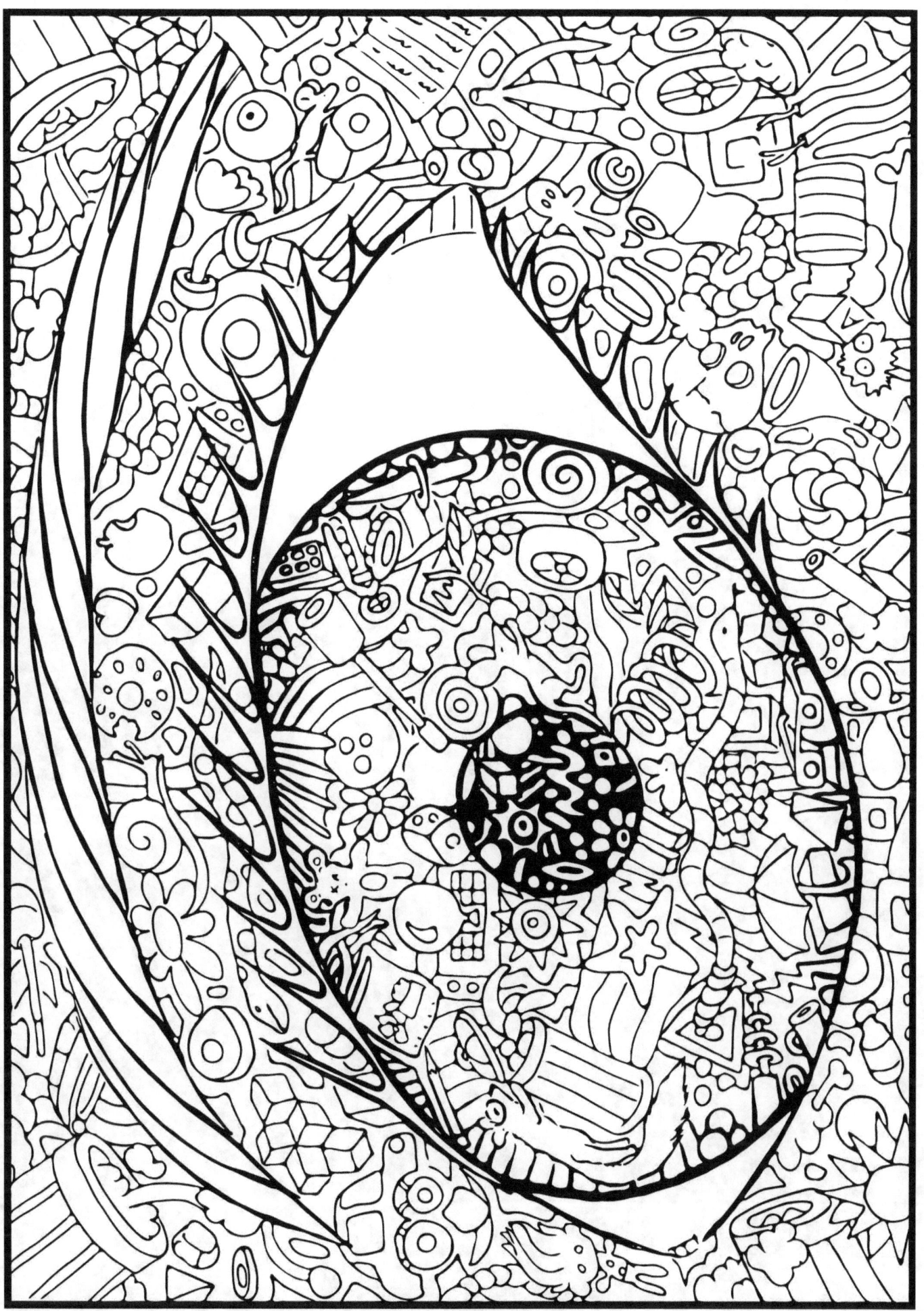

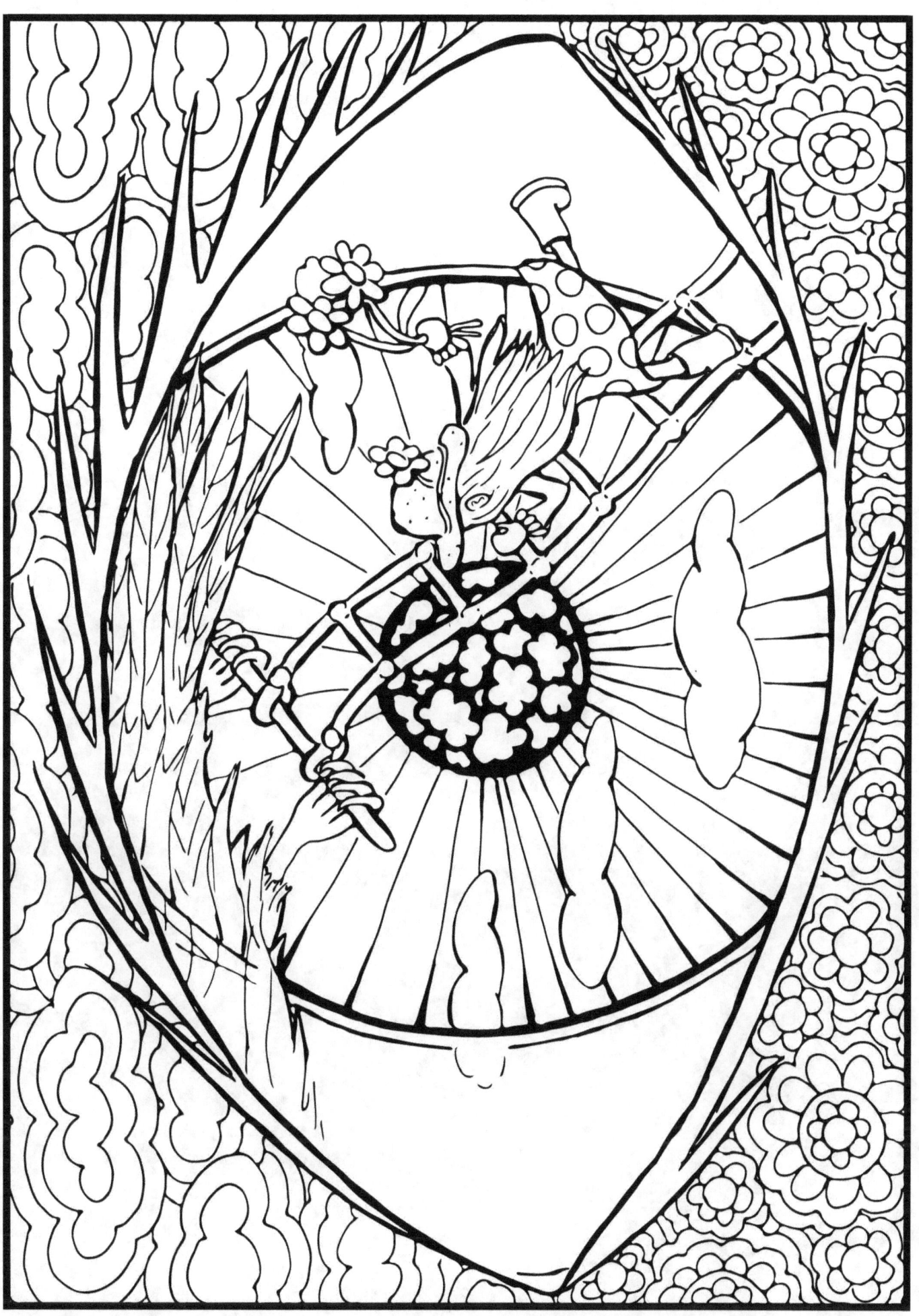

BONUS HALF PAGE VERSIONS START HERE!

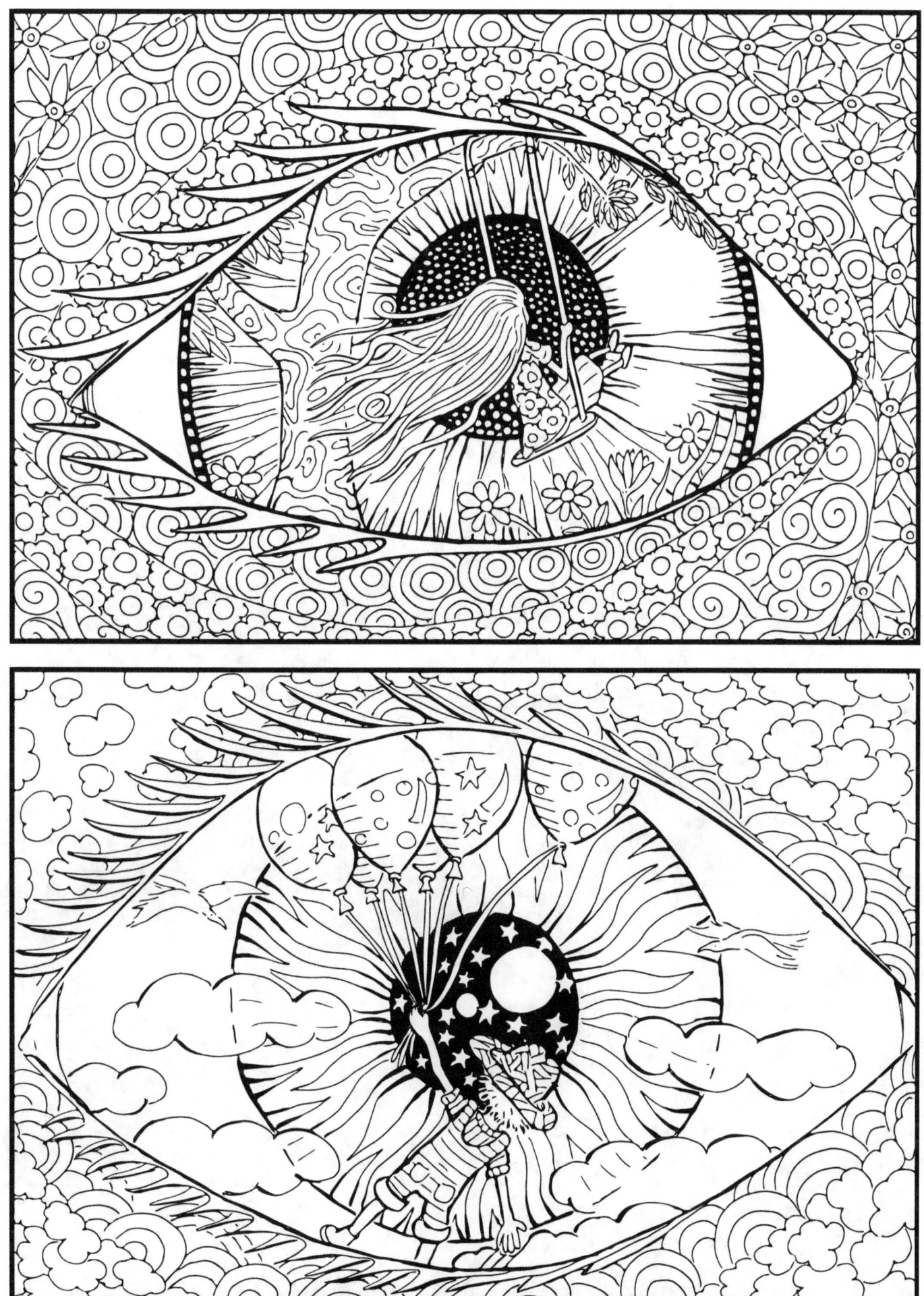

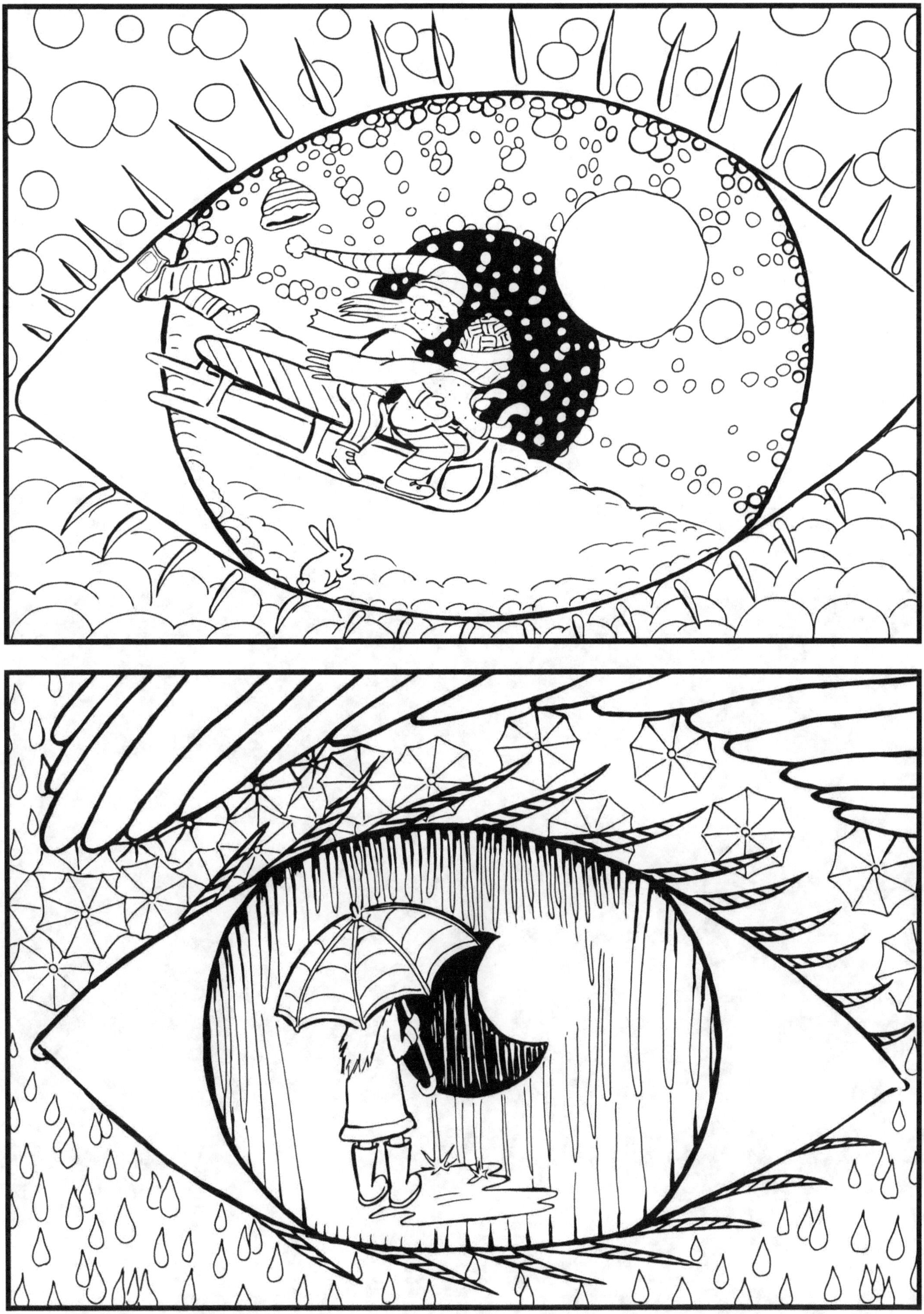

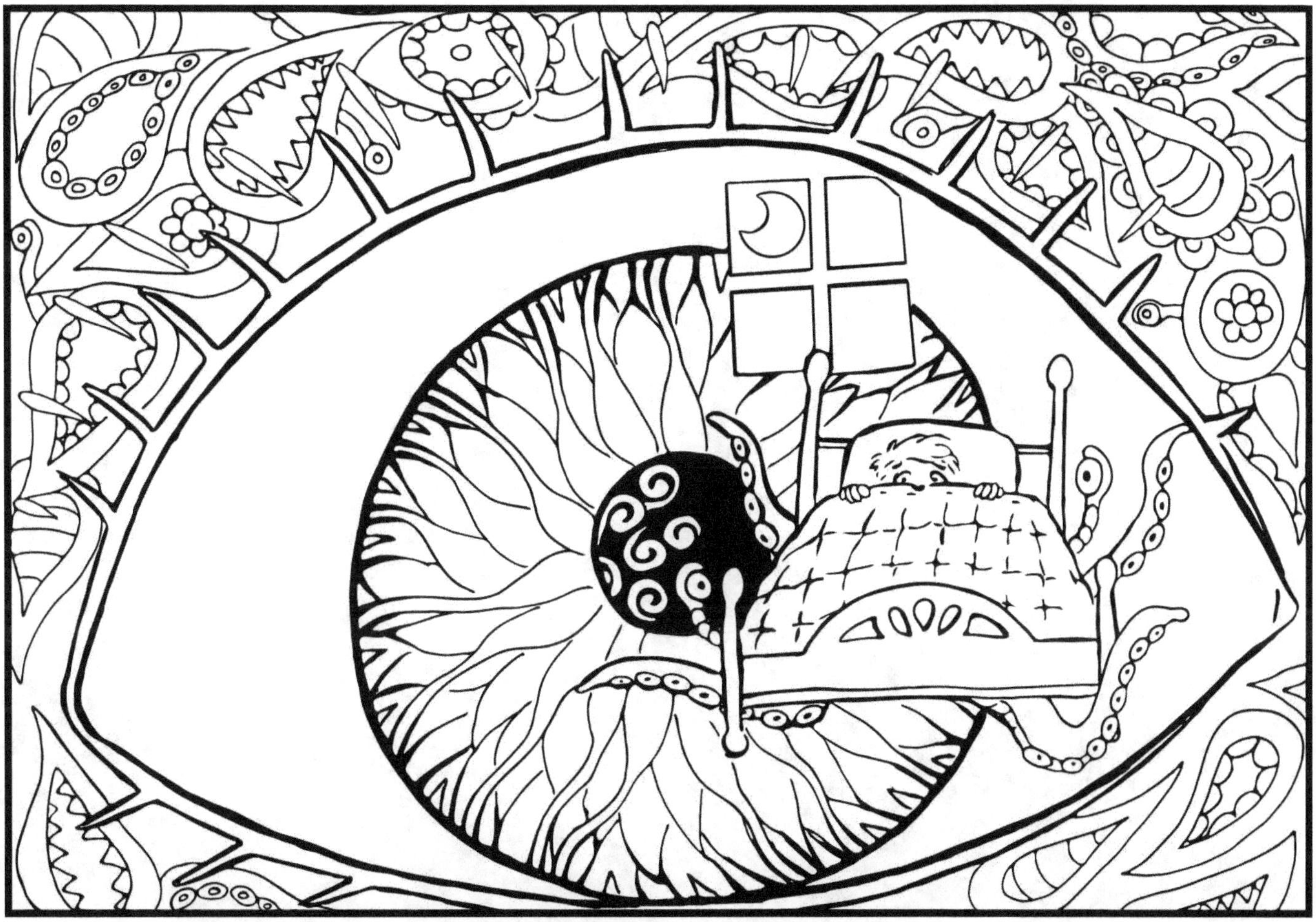

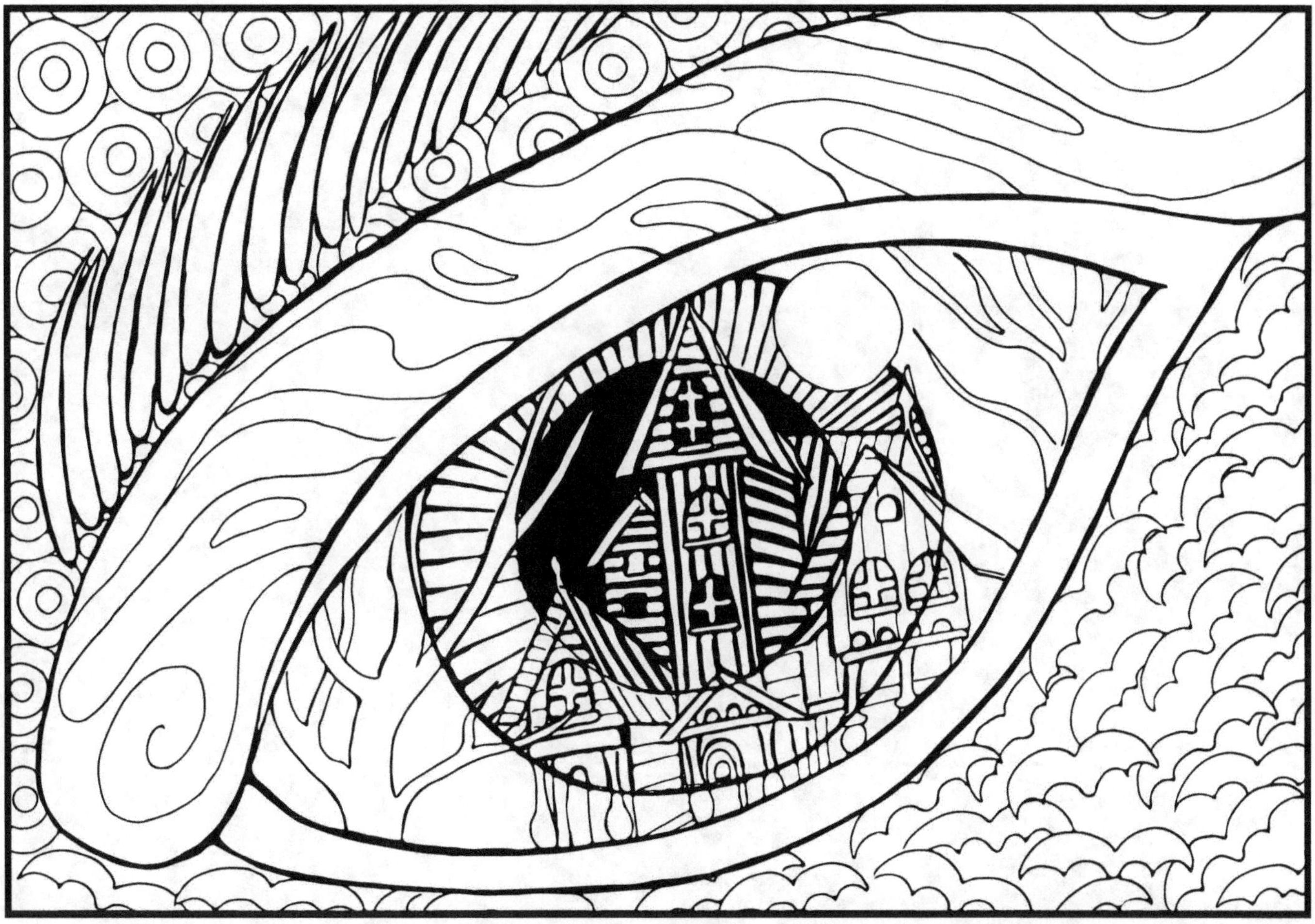

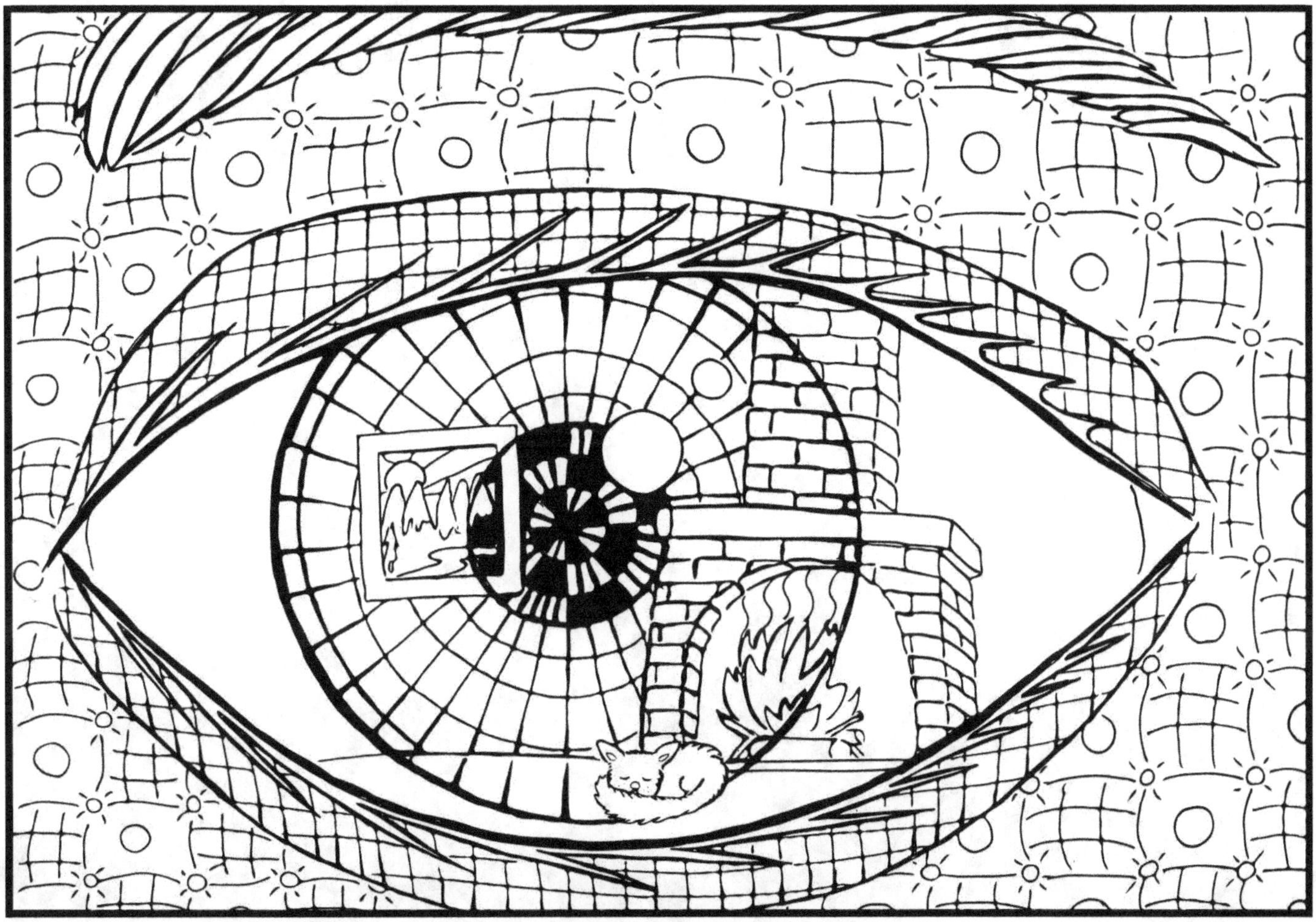

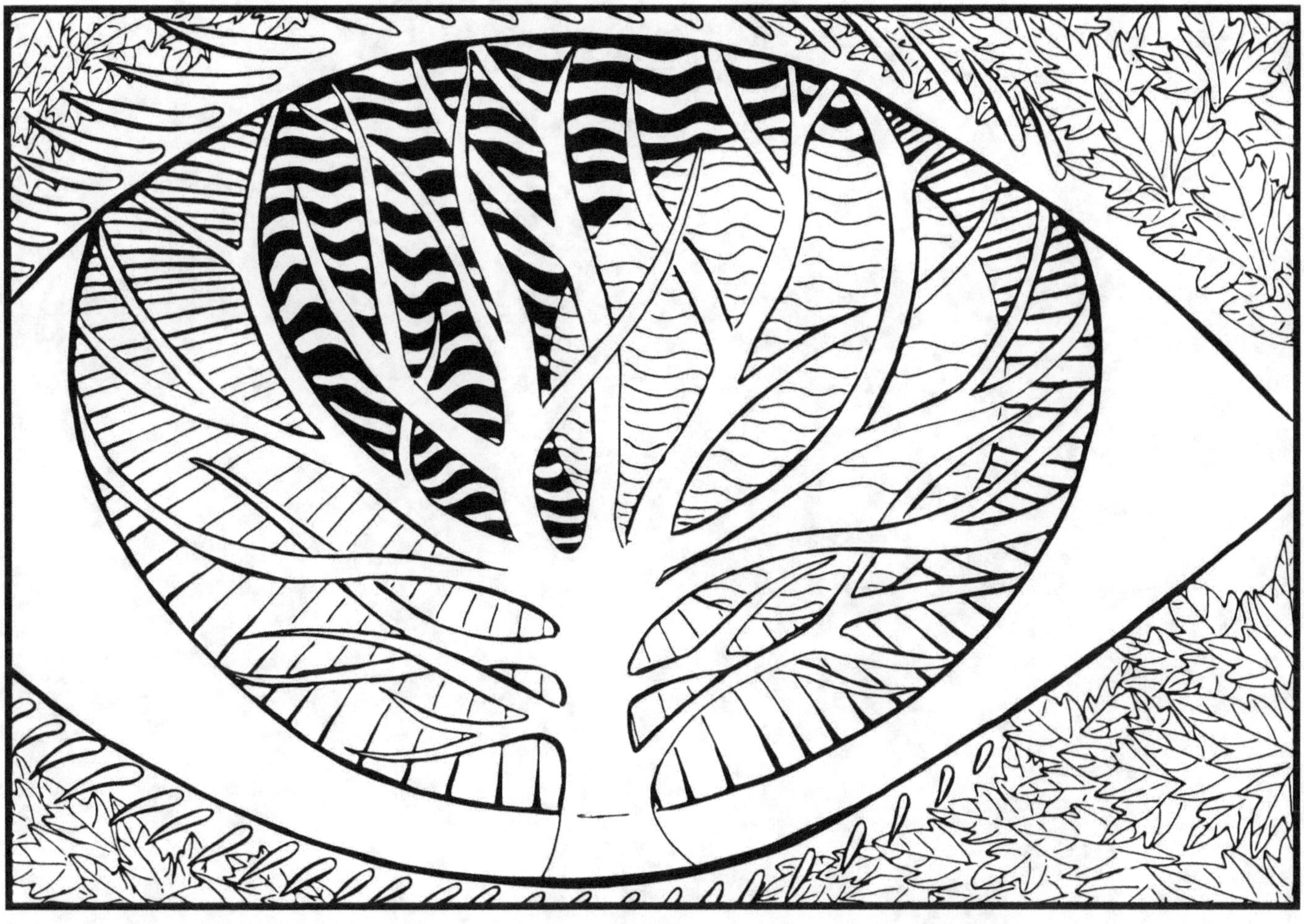

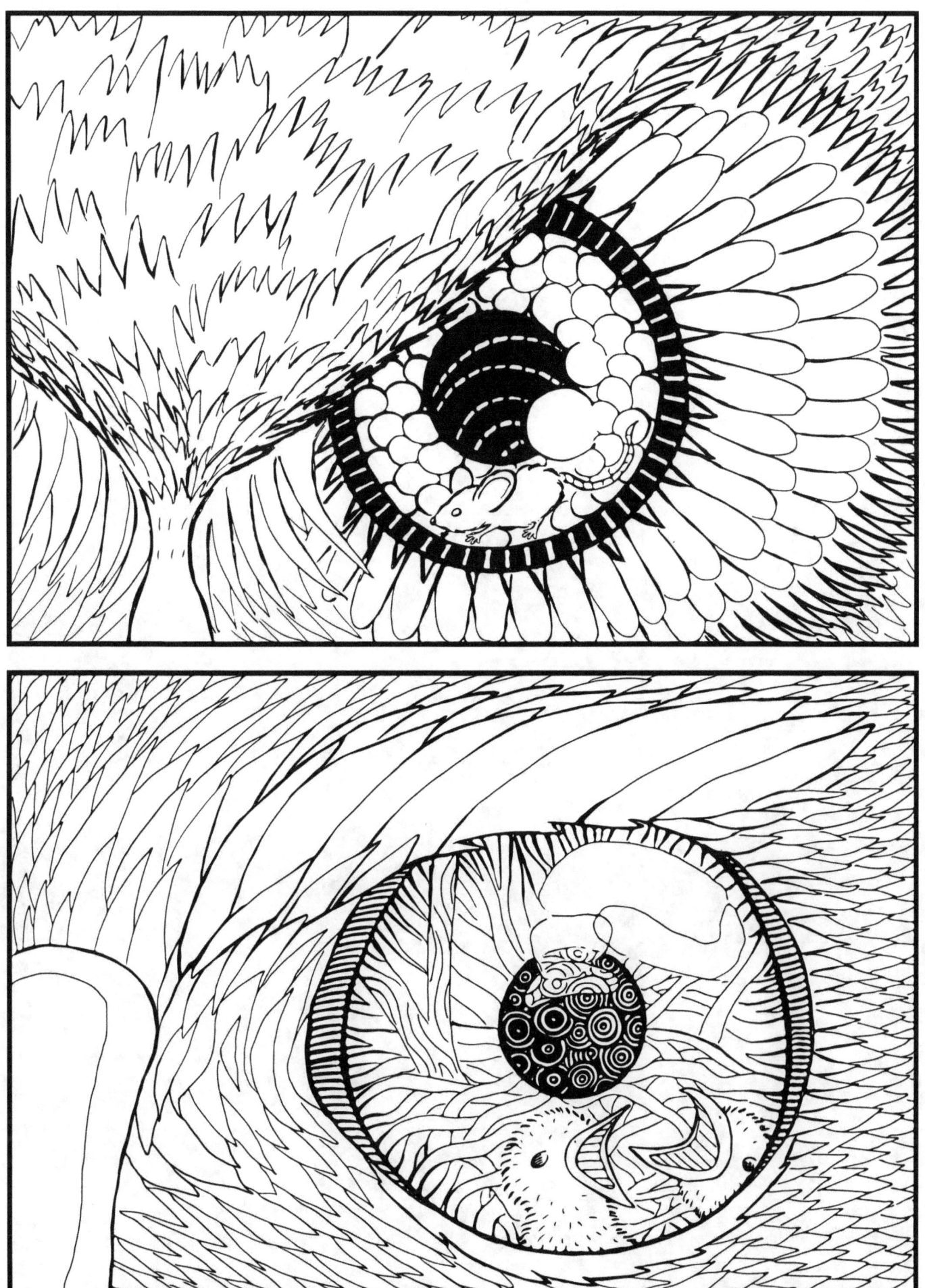

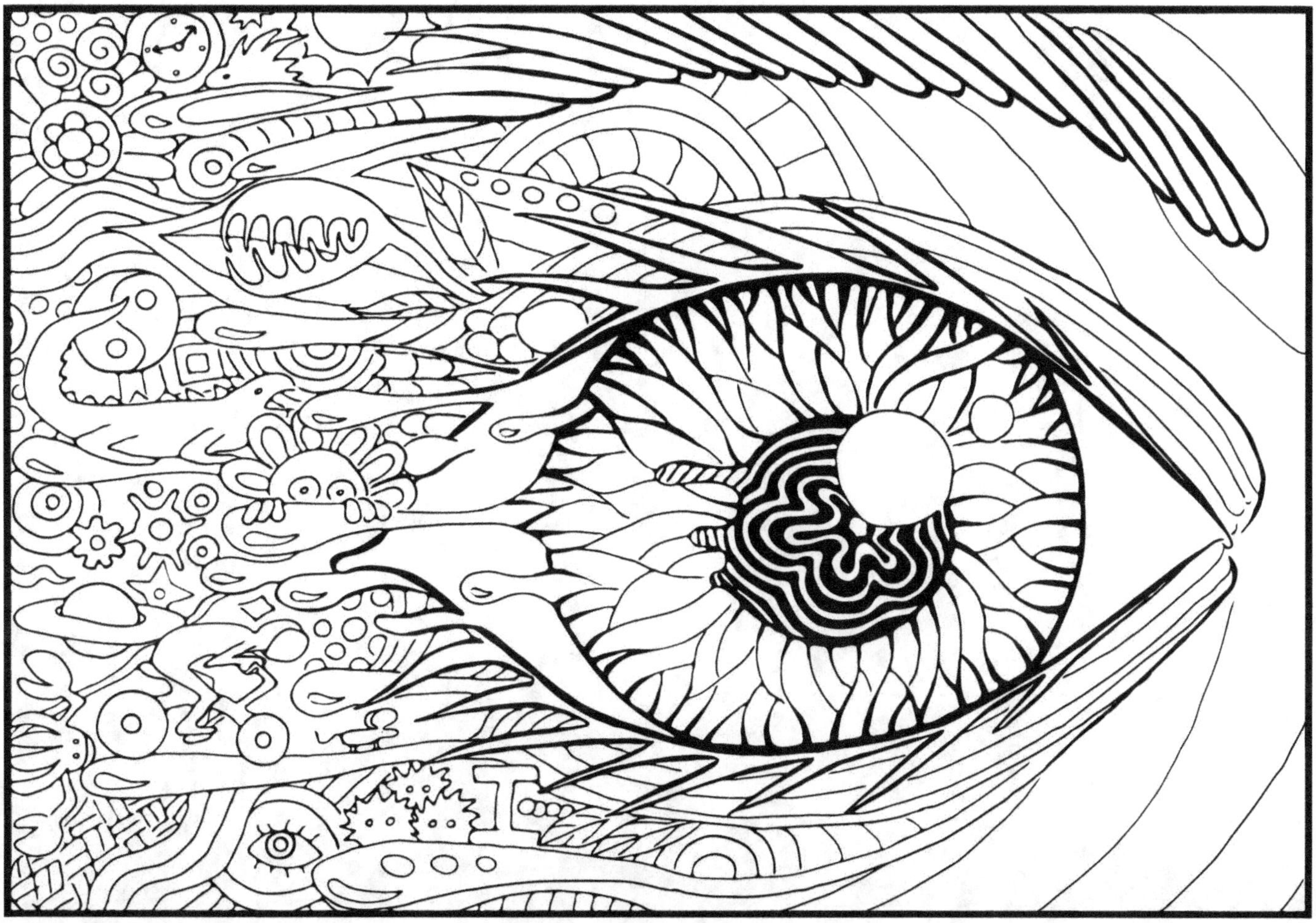

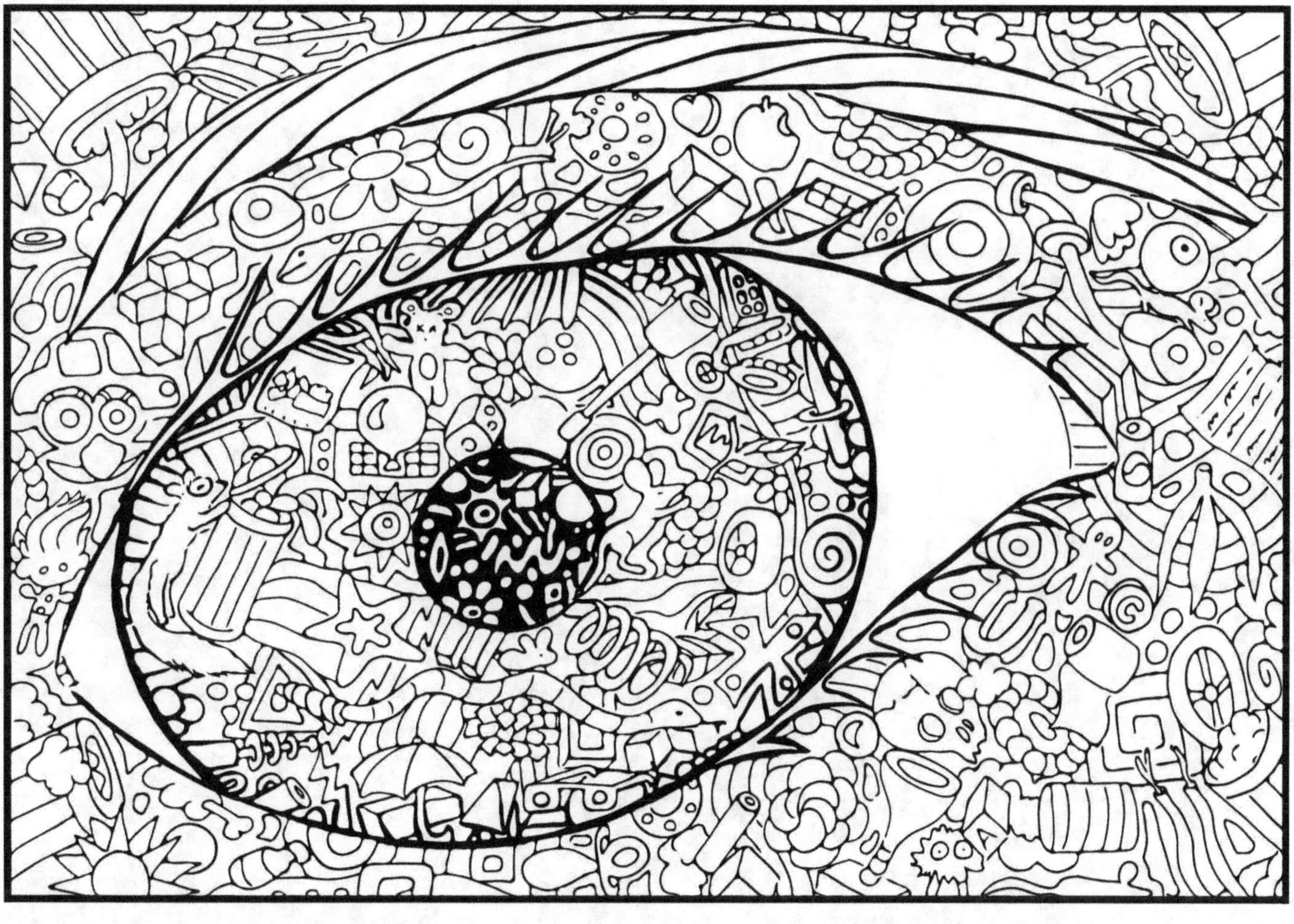

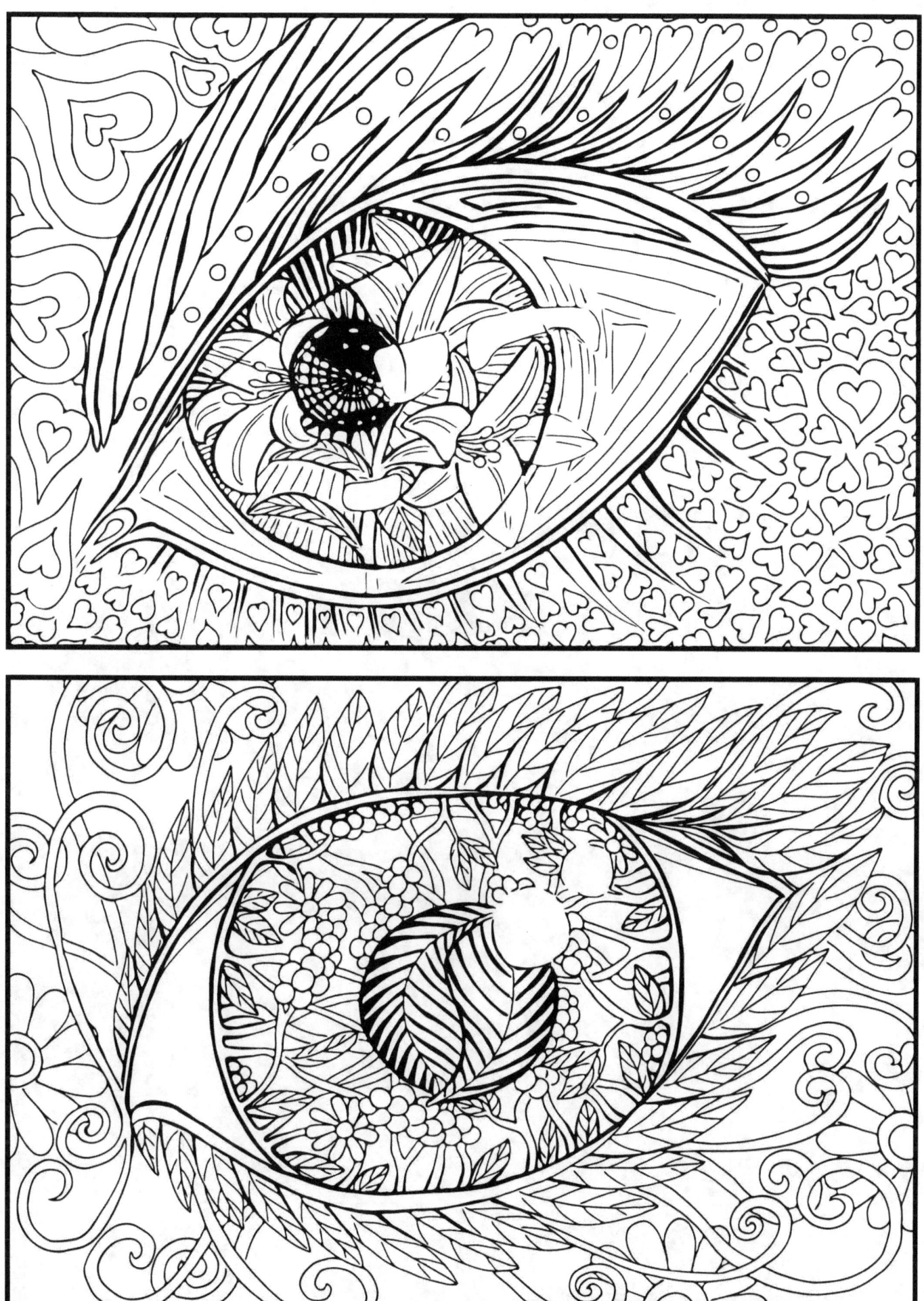

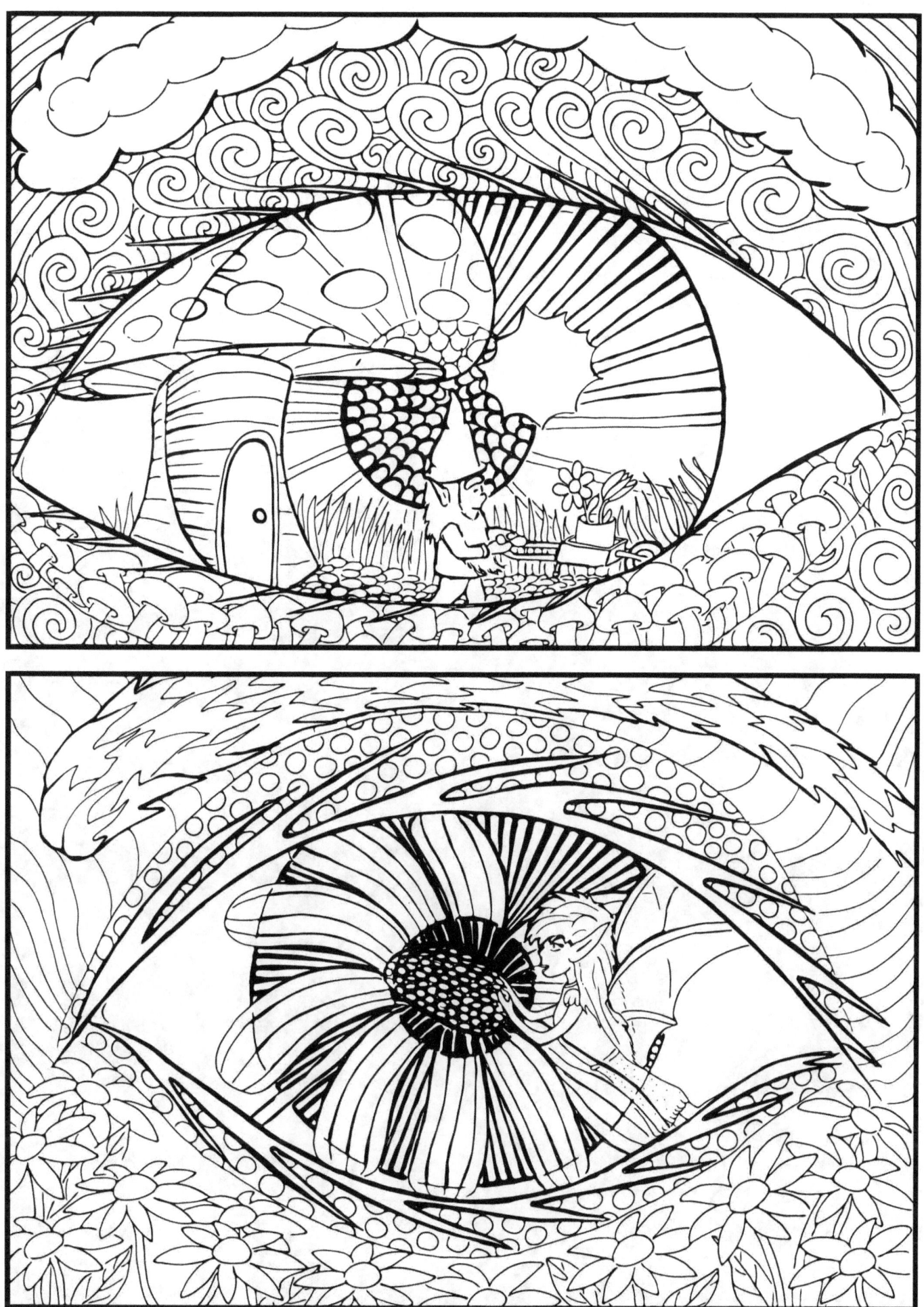

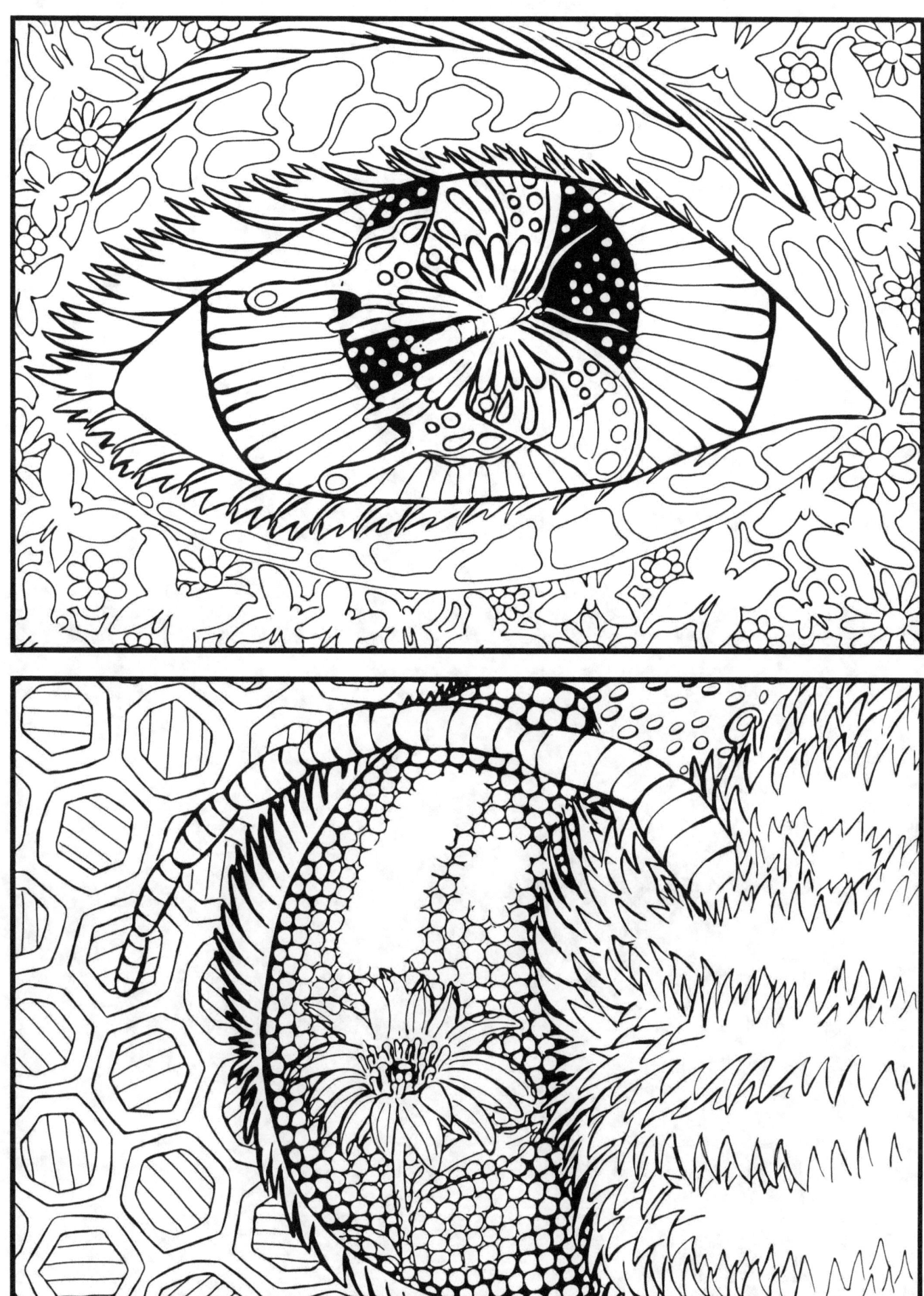

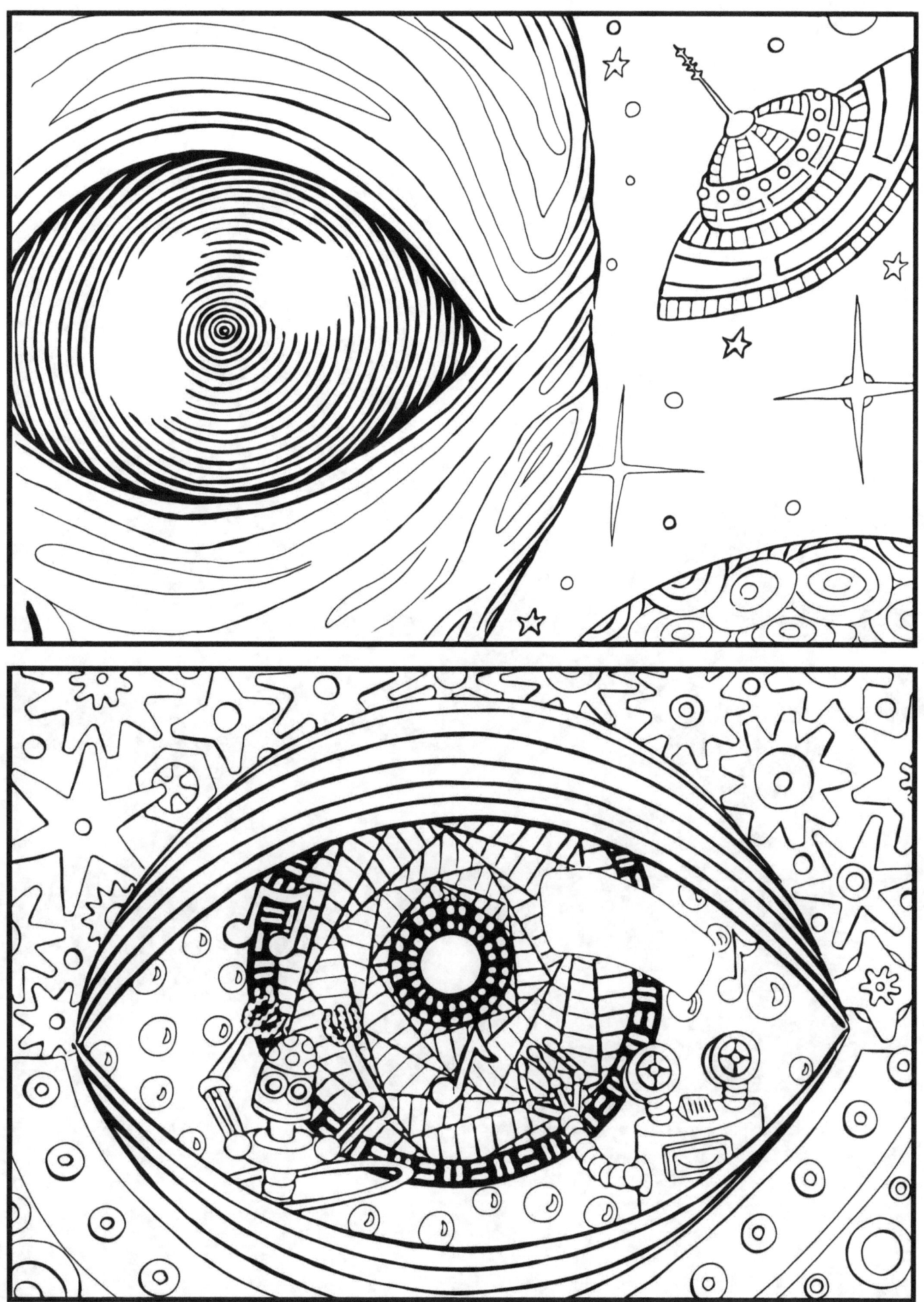

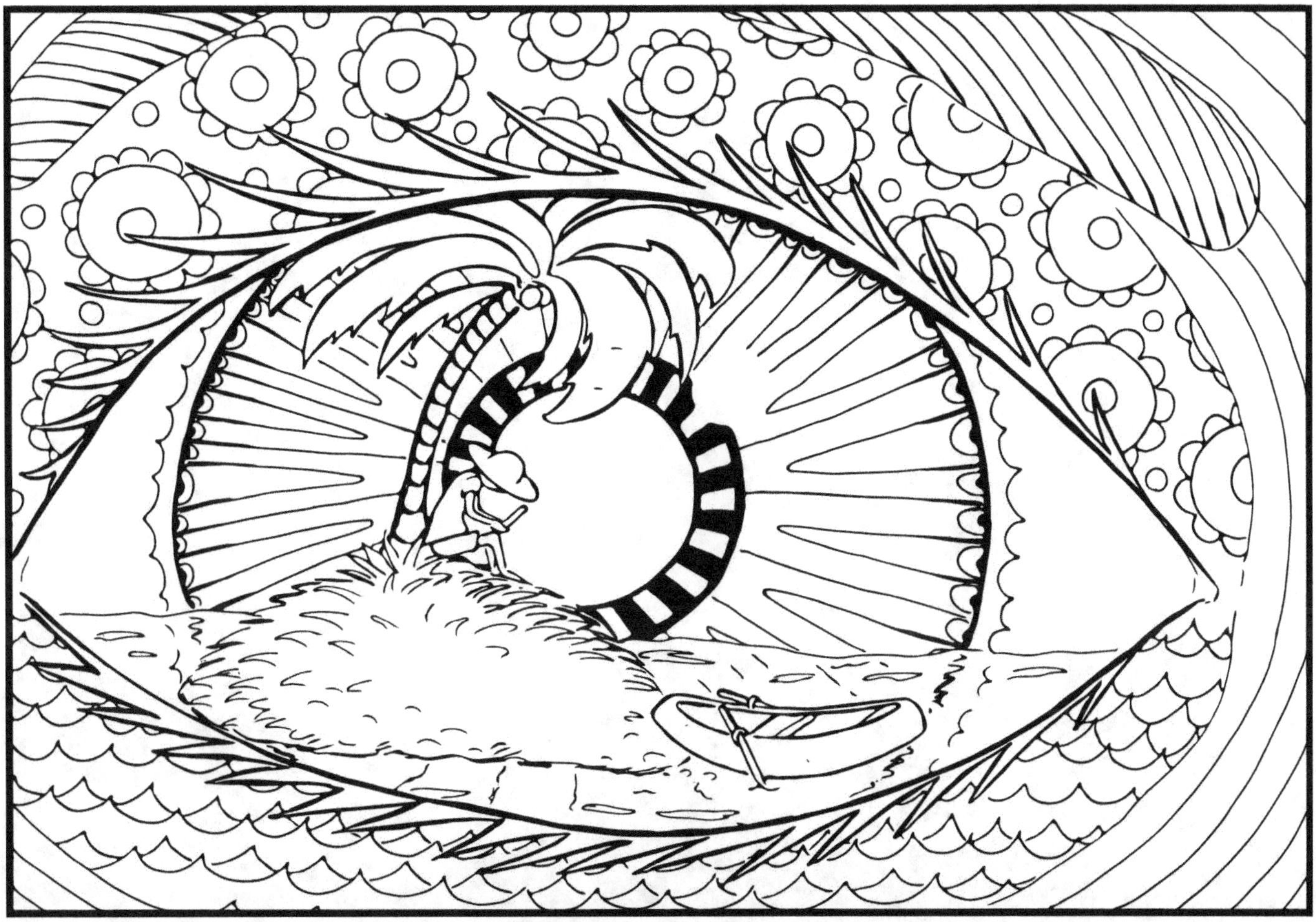

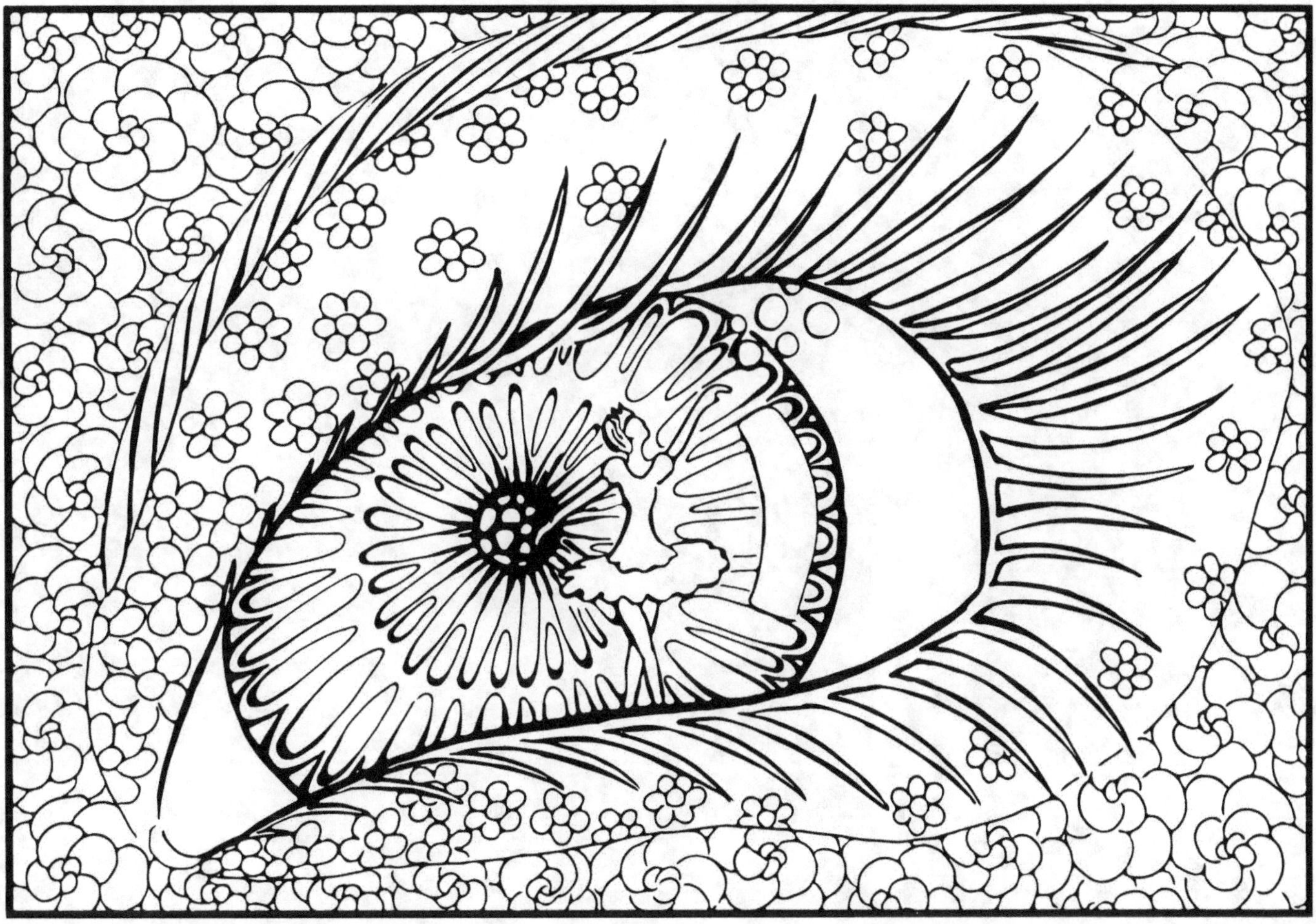

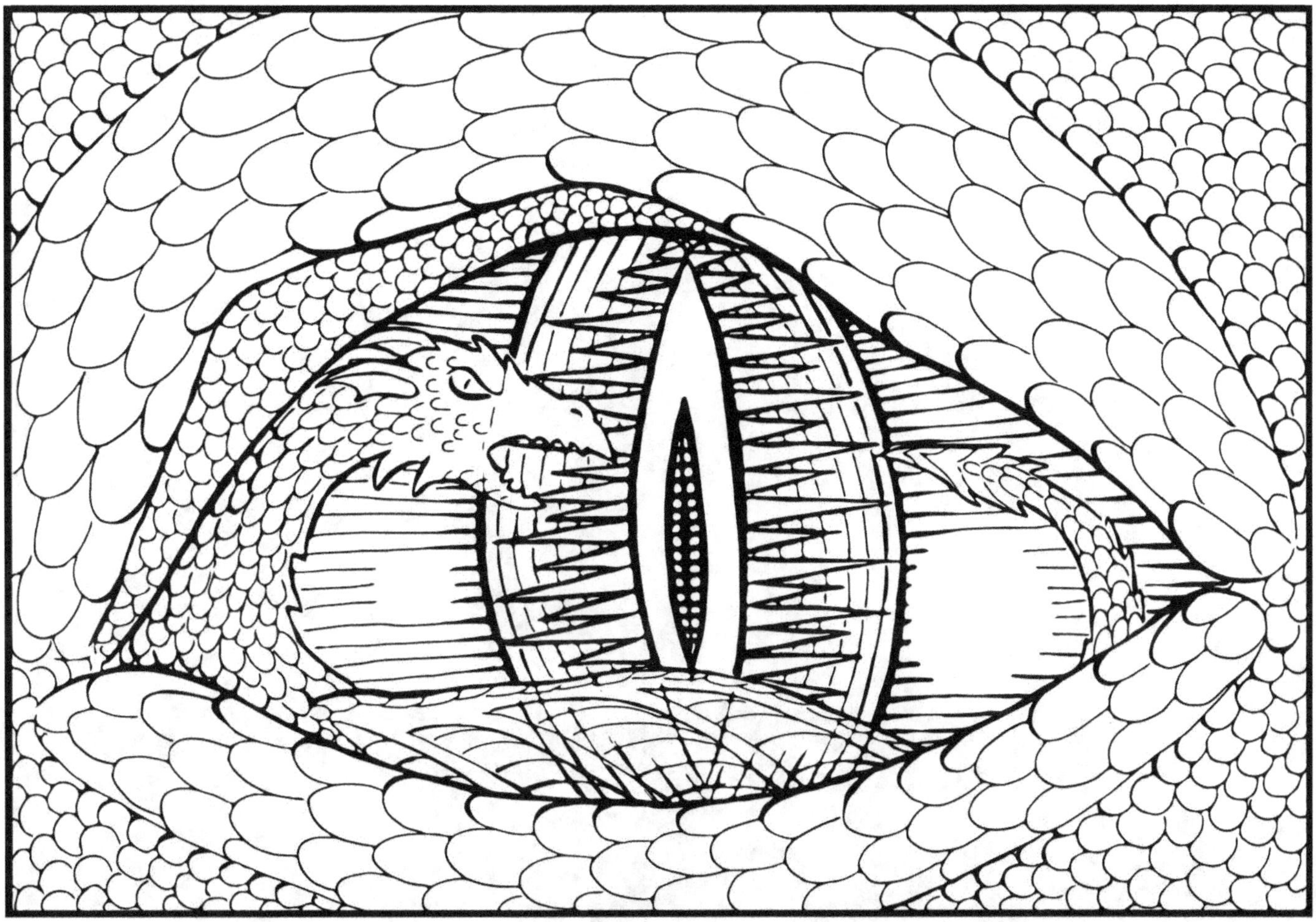
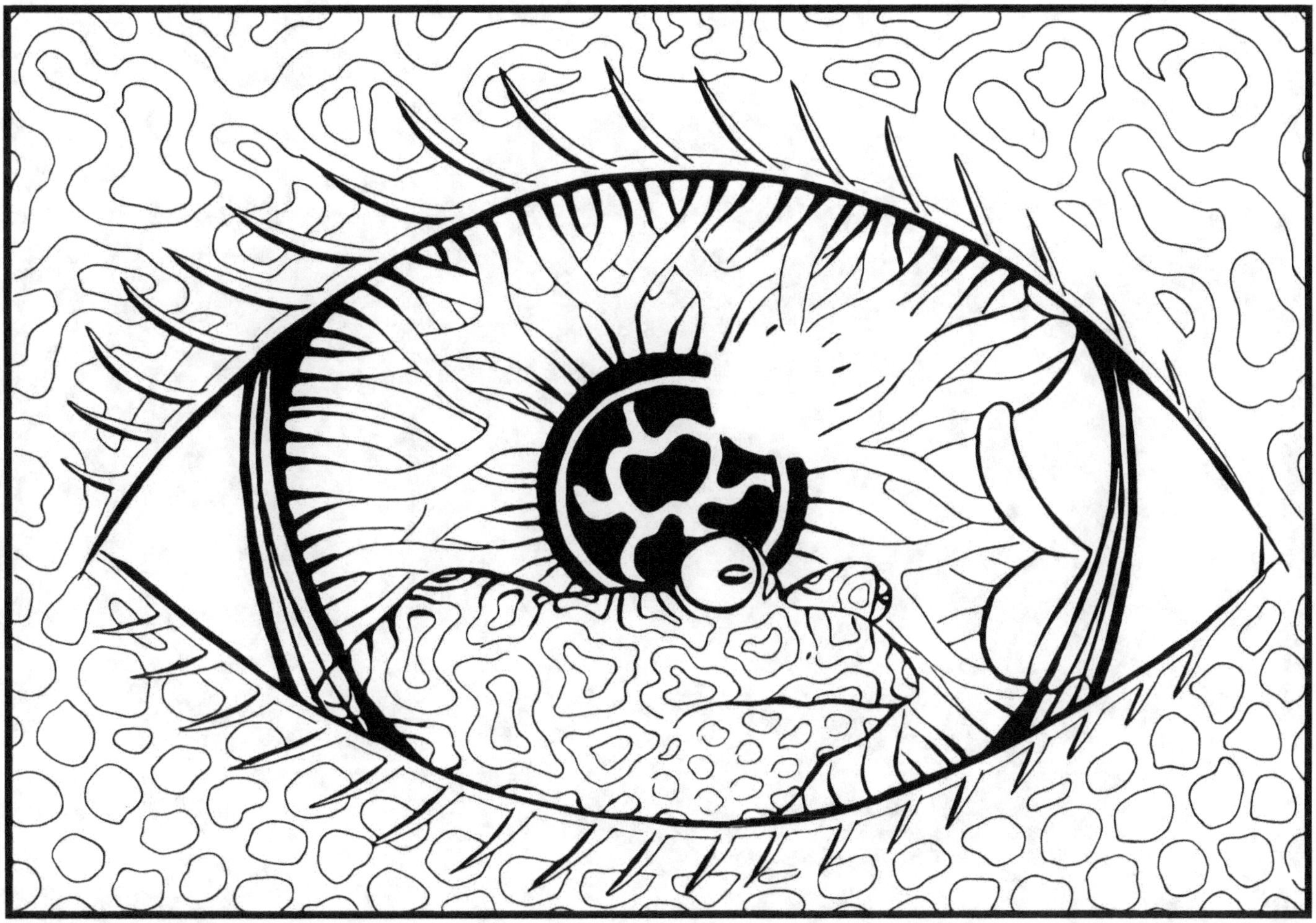

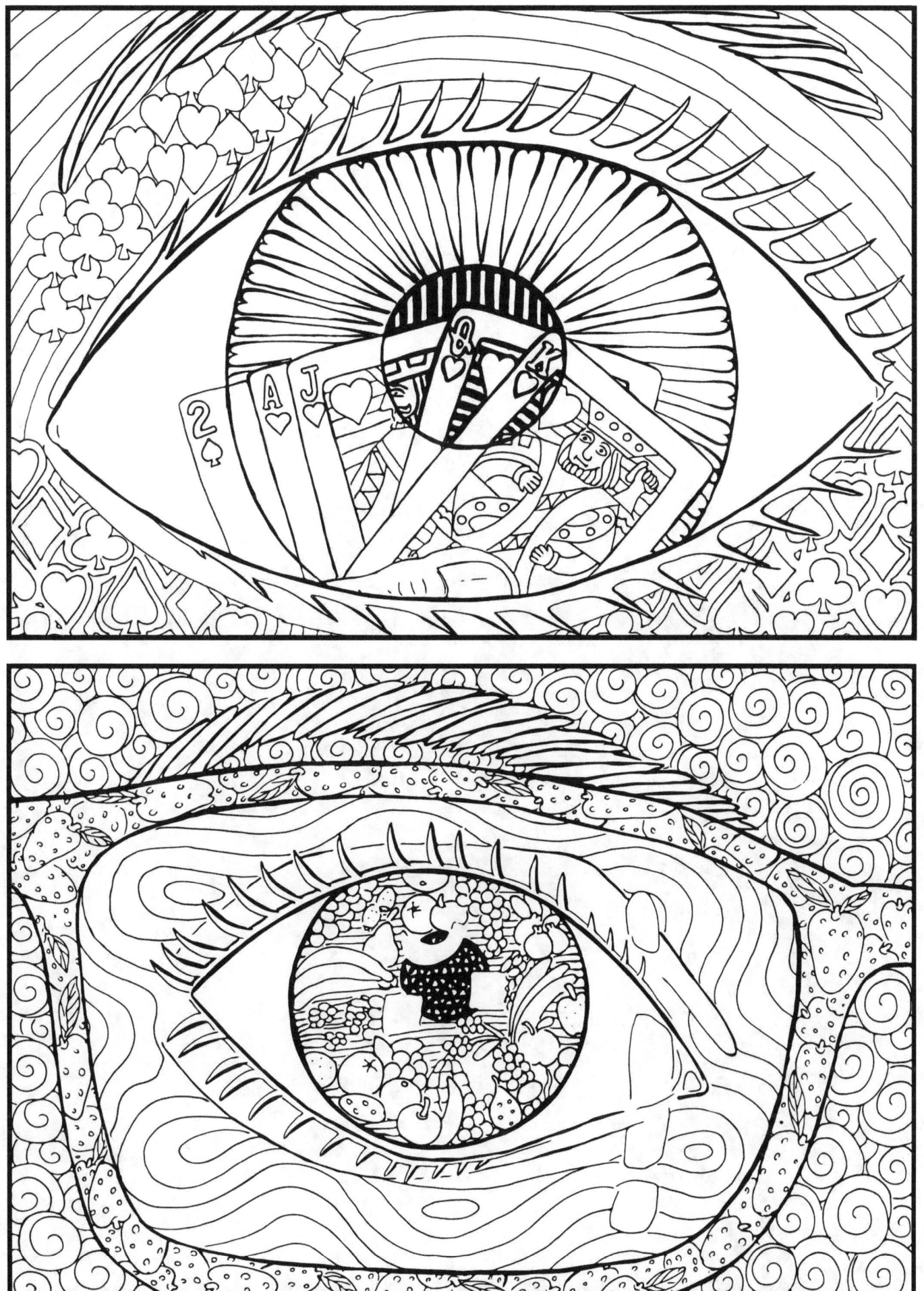

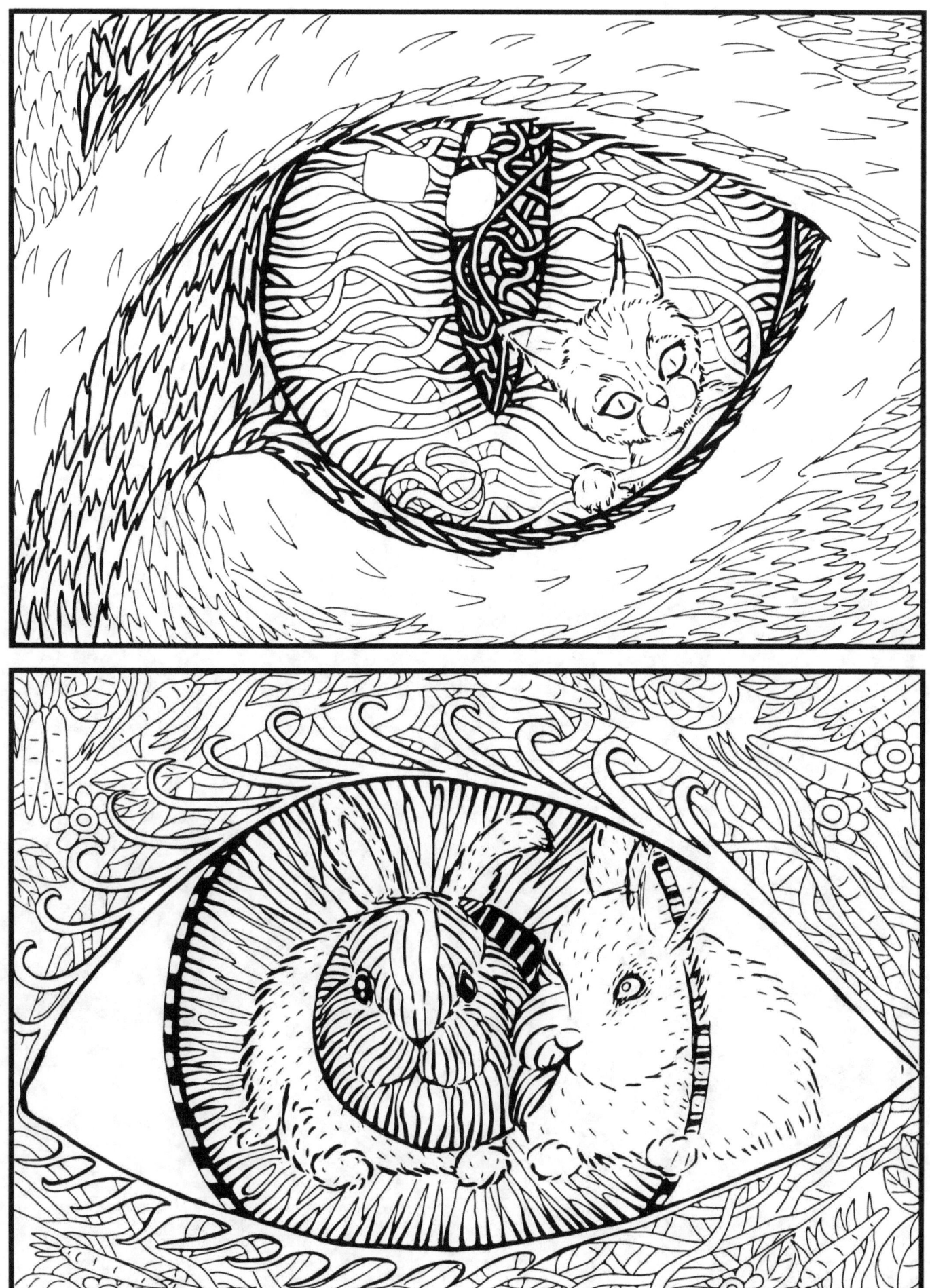

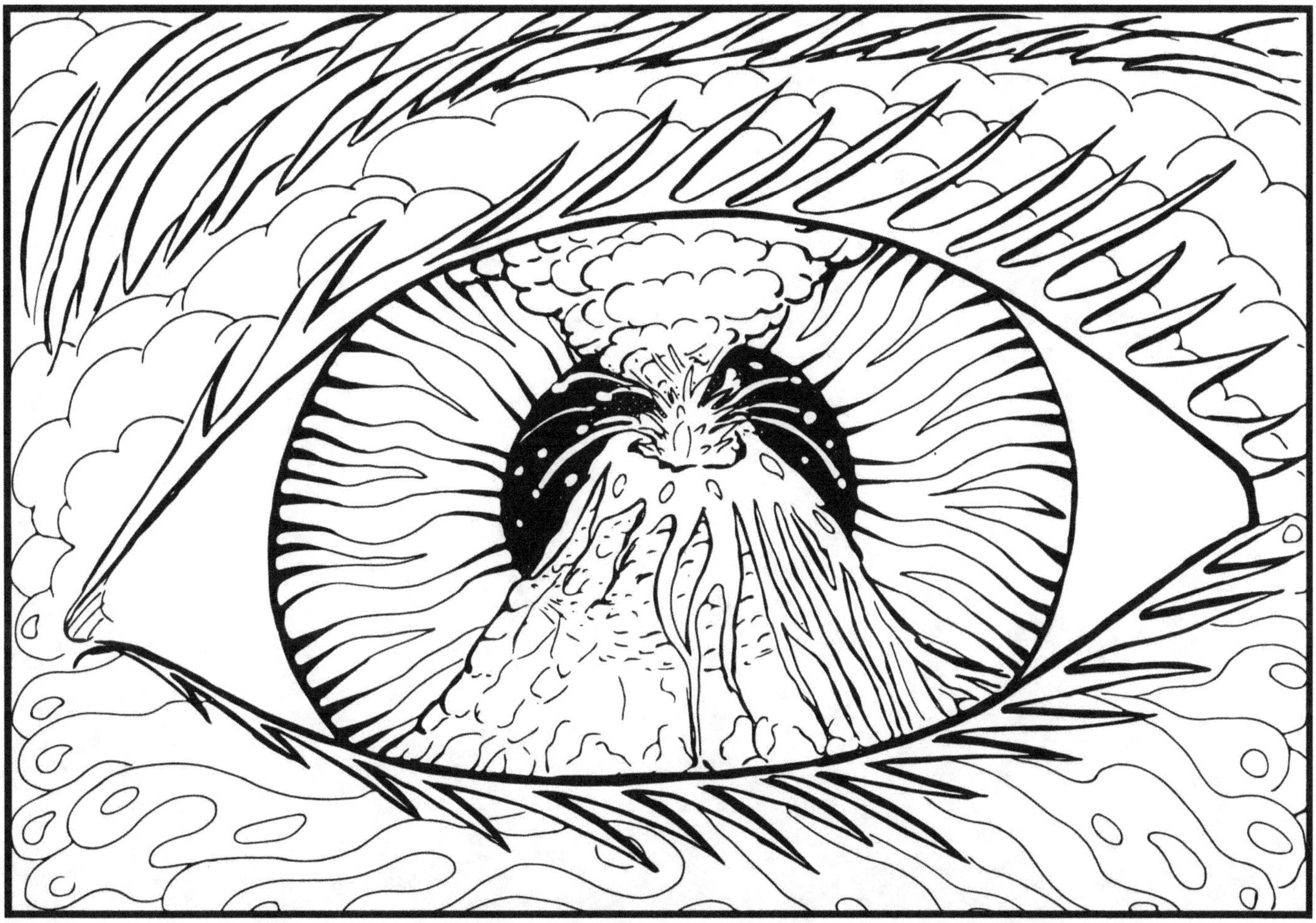

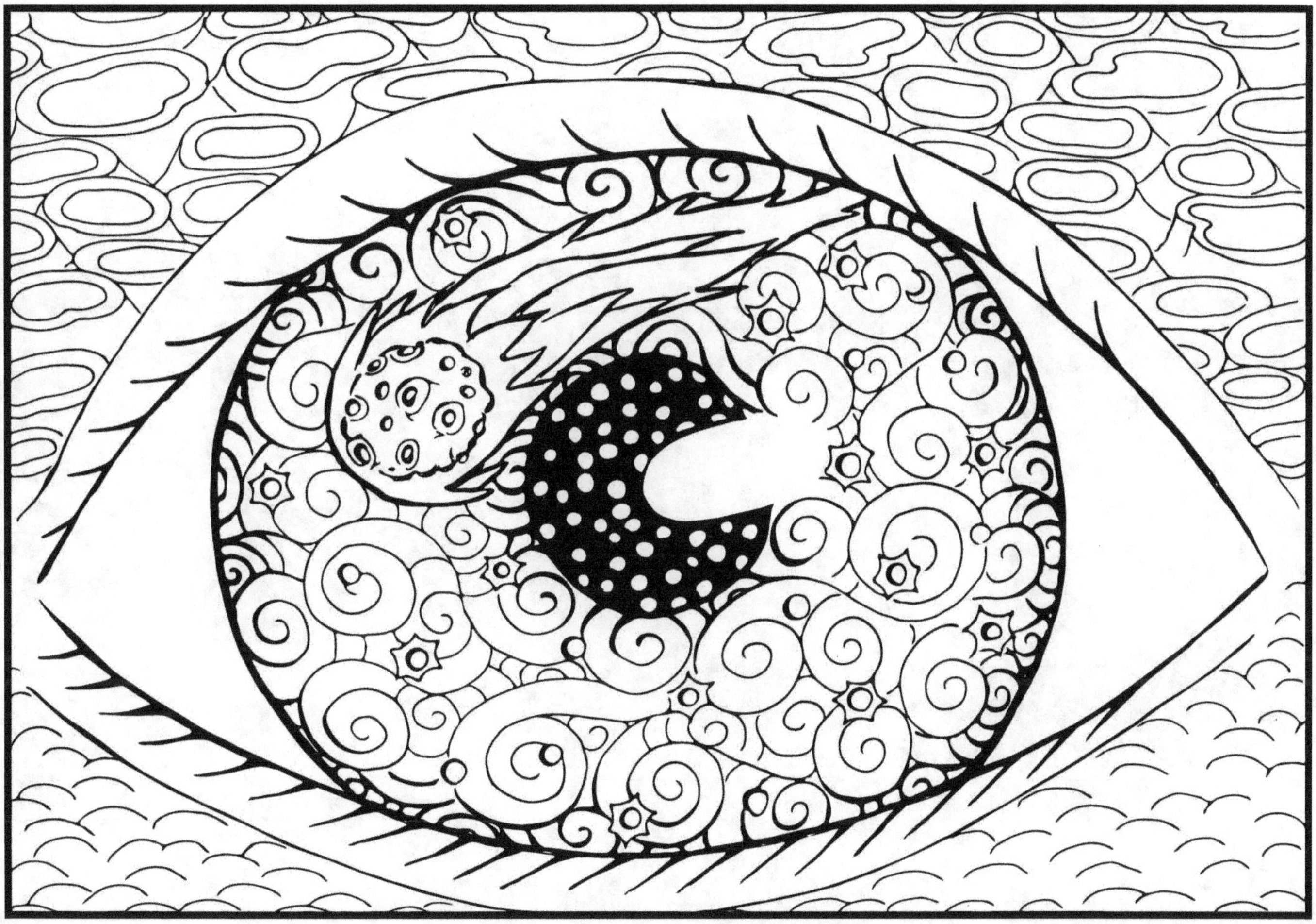

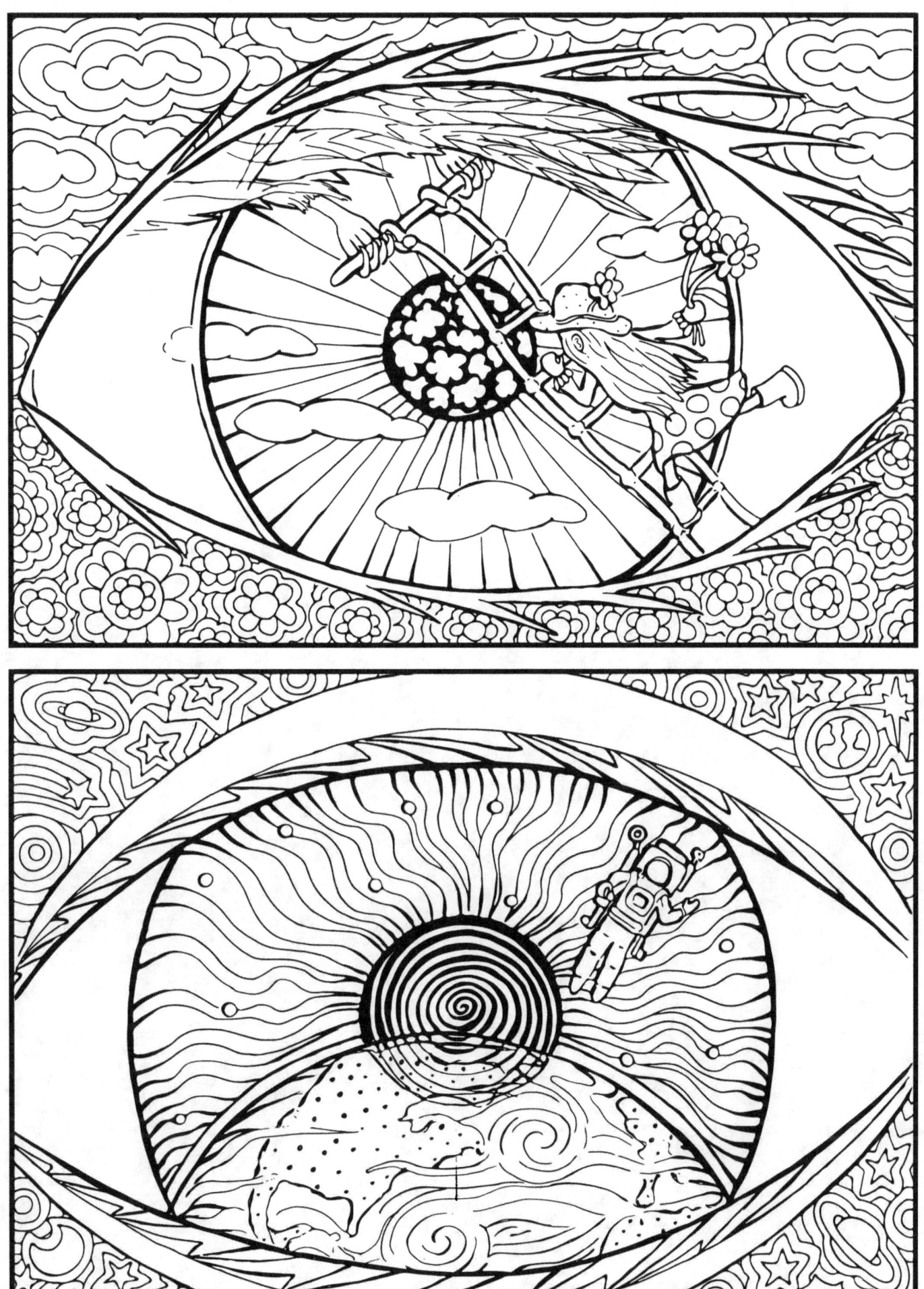

TEST AREA

Use this page to test out your colors and the way your media interacts with the paper.

Please check out these cool optical illusion
coloring books illustrated by me ('Trick):

Multiview Illusions Coloring Book

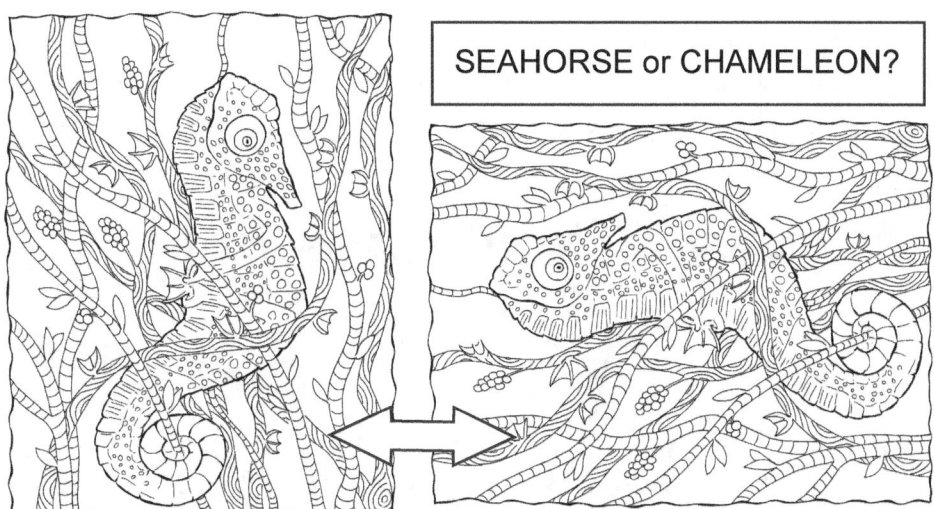

SEAHORSE or CHAMELEON?

25 ambiguous optical illusions that can be seen on more
than one way, depending on how you view the illusion.
These illusions have been duplicated so you can color the
other view or have a second chance.

Fantasy Flip Faces - Optical Illusions Coloring Book

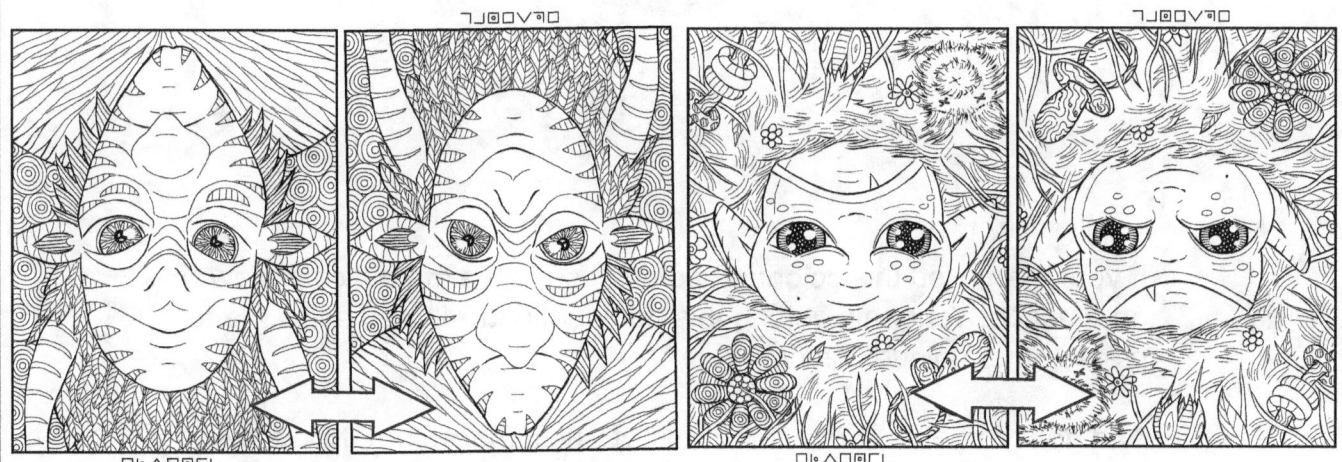

Save Terraflippia by coloring in these 25 fantasy flip face
ambiguous optical illusions that can be seen differently with
a flip of the page. These illusions have been duplicated so
you can color the other view or have a second chance.

For free coloring pages, coloring book updates,
secret pages, and artwork by me ('Trick) visit

www.TricksPlace.com

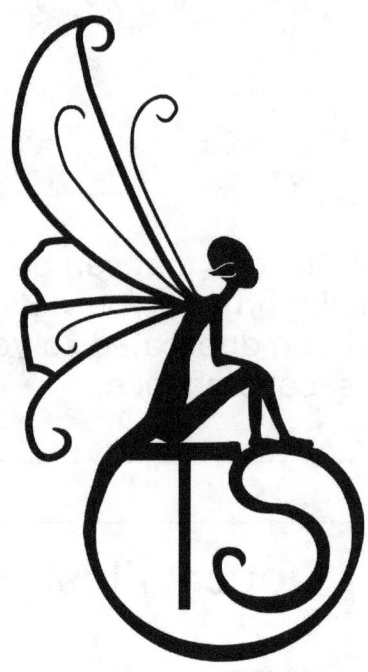

If you've enjoyed this coloring book please leave me a nice review
on Amazon! Your help getting this book noticed will also allow me to
create other unique coloring books.

And don't forget to connect with me at TricksPlace.com, follow me
on facebook.com/tricksplace/ and also join the facebook group
dedicated to sharing colored in pages from my books or website:
Facebook.com/groups/TricksPlaceColoring/

#tricksplace #eyecoloring